*Inter Arma Enim S*ɩ ᵨes:
Defending Latin America's
Military Governments

Matthew Raphael Johnson

Hromada Books
2019

Preface

As always, this paper is written with no institutional support. I'm on my own. While it allows me free speech and unimpeded research, its also kept me quite poor. The right is overtly oppressed in this country. Our Facebook pages are deleted, our journals have credit cards taken from them, we lose jobs and are kicked out of universities for no other reason than we're on the right of the political spectrum. This is the very definition of oppression.

I've dedicated my life to exposing these elites, their arrogance and stupidity. Professors and businessmen pretend their independent actors, but they're scared children, afraid of being called names on the internet.

This book is dedicated to everyone who has lost a job, marriage or social status based on belief. In this case, its true belief. I don't demand "freedom of speech" on abstract grounds, only on the grounds that the Right is correct both factually and in interpretation. This is why the Left functions by threats and violence without exception.

I've lost lucrative teaching jobs for no reason other than I'm one of these accursed people. Never was my ability, intelligence or originality brought into question. In fact, I was the most popular professor in Mount Saint Mary's history without doubt. The fear is so great that they'd risk student anger rather than keep me on. When I was fired, 181 students signed an angry petition demanding my return. They were ignored.

The Left knows right wing views only in caricature. It knows strawman descriptions that they pat themselves on the back for rejecting. Academia is stagnating to the point of crisis due to ideological fear and the rule of women, who can get a student or professor fired by even an indirect accusation of some wrongdoing. Women are automatically hired for academic positions regardless of knowledge or ability and, vaguely aware of their illegitimate position, rule the university with an iron hand. This is called "Impostor Syndrome" in the psychological literature.

My resentment and contempt for this ruling class knows no bounds for this reason. Error, stupidity and illogic are enshrined in law and "common sense" by lawmakers, journalists and professors that know how silly their views are.

Their day is coming.

MRJ
Johnstown, PA
June 14 2019

Table of Contents:

Chapter 1.
Introduction

Newly elected President Jair Bolsonaro has expressed admiration for Brazil's period of military rule. He's come under withering media criticism for it. Unfortunately for them, he's right. Without exception, the American and European press has attacked every move he's made from the first few hours of his term. He's a "far right fringe" figure, a phrase every major American media outlet uses, proving they've, as always, coordinated their "reporting." Bolsonaro is a former army officer, which itself makes him suspicious and the terminology used to describe his most innocuous policy interests can only be described as hysterical.

The Washington Post calls him a "hard right nationalist" who "rode a wave of rage" to the Presidency. Still, Bolsonaro advocates for global free trade. This means the *Post* is unaware of what "nationalism" is and is likely using the term to frighten its rapidly dwindling readership. The *Post* says "He demonized opponents and polarized the nation with his history of denigrating women, gays and minorities." They were short on specifics, but also ran another article entitled, "How Jair Bolsonaro Entranced

Brazil's Minorities — While Also Insulting Them."
Something's not quite right here. Black voters were a key
part of Bolsonaro's election victory.

Like Latin American since the Second World War,
liberal democracy has led to the utter destruction of the
local economy. Under Brazil's Leftist banana republic,
2018 saw the murder of almost 70,000 people. The *Post*
tells us that his "tough on crime" approach – as if he has a
choice – will fall on poor areas that are mostly black.
Hence, while blacks love him because he promised to kill
the drug dealers, they really hate him – we're told – because
most of these dealers are black. This is the level of logic in
American journalism today.

It is a common claim that the United States
"supported brutal" militarist governments in Latin America
in the 20th century because they were "anti-communist." It
is repeated so often that no one, not even conservatives,
challenge it. As always with such proverbial wisdom, it's
false. There's no reason to believe these military
governments were particularly brutal in the context of civil
wars and guerrilla insurgencies. Further, they came into
existence because weak republics failed to deal with the
disintegration of the country in almost all cases. Since both

academia and journalism are Leftist activist centers, their ideological assumptions distort their perceptions and reason. Brazil elected what the system calls a "nationalist" for the same reason South Americans welcomed military leadership in their countries: liberalism destroyed them, and the normal manifestation of liberalism is democratic capitalism.

The third world is a closed book to Americans and what little they know is a poorly reasoned set of myths. Military governments in Latin America engaged in the most far reaching land reform programs possible at the time. Democratically elected governments in the 20th century did not and could not. Soldiers are usually from the peasant classes and have their own sources of funding. They can go over the heads of the wealthy. Its these very same rich, often foreign, elites that politicians must court in all democratic elections. Politicians do not have independent sources of funding except in very rare cases. Bolsonaro doesn't have the advantages of a military dictator and his interest in "free trade" is proof of this. He's already setting the groundwork for the privatization of Brazil's ports that the military nationalized many decades ago.

The US opposed military governments on principle

and sought to promote non-communist, but certainly liberal, parties and movements. It was no different in El Salvador, Cuba and anywhere a military government ruled during the Cold War. Military governments usually come into existence at the 11th hour to stop their society's descent into madness and many have ideologies almost never described even in specialized studies. In brief, they are national socialists in the most general sense of the term. They seek a strong state that can run a growing economy while ensuring a more or less fair distribution of goods and a purely national economic plan. This is done under the most harsh circumstances.

Civil war, outdated transportation systems, poor infrastructure, drug problems, foreign pressure and budgetary wretchedness make even the best intentioned ruler willing to do almost anything to save his country. That is, unless he's being rewarded to maintain its condition, as Dependency Theory wisely makes clear. Yet none of this is taken into account by a journalist class that has convinced itself "democracy dies in darkness." They are the darkness.

Some of the more absurd claims are that, speaking of the anti-communist movements in the area, "According to John Henry Coatsworth, a historian of Latin America and the provost of Columbia University [as if this adds weight to his analysis], the number of victims in Latin America alone far surpassed that of the Soviet Union and the Eastern Bloc during the period 1960 to 1990."

Coatsworth, perpetually the propagandist, thinks that de-Stalinization meant the dismantling of the GULags. Rather, the percentage of the Soviet economy dependent on slave labor actually increased. Khrushchev was no different from Stalin, Lenin or Trotsky. He just had slightly better PR and a far more advanced state apparatus. The Soviet Gulag population in this period was several million, with about 30 million in China and a large portion of the population in Cambodia. His statement is laughably false.

"Operation Condor" is often cited as evidence, though most of this evidence is circumstantial and the number of deaths (indirectly) attributed to it are grossly inflated. Yet even if they were not, these nations were in the midst of civil wars. Keep in mind that Pol Pot and Mao were in power as these Leftist guerrillas were being fought in Latin America. The nations involved had much to lose if they lost. The number of claimed victims of Operation Condor, allegedly a CIA plot to fight Marxism, were no more than 60,000, which is a very restrained number given multiple civil wars. 60,000 dead is a bad weekend for Lenin. Condor was a US supported movement, as we're told, to fight Marxism that stretched from the Johnson to Reagan Administrations.

The truth is that Condor was the creation of the militaries of the area to assist one another in fighting both Marxism and drug trafficking. While the Left had cocaine dealers, Cuba and the USSR, the anti-communist movement needed an "international" of their own. This became, in the eyes of Leftist professors and journalists, a sinister set of "Operations" that sound like they come from a James Bond film. This is because for the most part, they do. They tap into the popular ignorance. From there, confident that countervailing information will be absent, they can spin the tale of "supporting death squads" and other Hollywood PR slogans.

Declassified documents include the formerly secret "Memorandum of Conversation" in Chile dated June 6 1976, document number 200202913. It is a conversation between Undersecretary Rogers and Foreign Minister Guzzetti of Argentina, among others. This document doesn't mention any operation and is primarily concerned with the effect of terrorism on Americans living in the country. Marxism isn't mentioned at all. It's rarely mentioned in other documents except when analyzing the mentality of the local militaries. As I've argued in many other places, "Marxism" was never the concern of the US. Nationalism was.

Another is a State Department Document called "The Third World War and Latin America" is from August 3 1976, number AO003A. It mentions Condor, but also says the militaries of the area are "paranoid" about Marxist subversion. It condemns the military in these areas for "bloody counter-terrorism" that "threatens to increase their isolation from the west." Condor is not said to be an American operation, but a local one. In contrast to what the Left believes, it condemns the military governments for veering into "national socialism" (page 6) and they should only be temporary. It makes the verifiable claim that the military has helped develop these countries substantially, but the "human rights" issue is a problem. They mock the military of Paraguay as a "19th century military regime that looks good on a cartoon page" (page 9). The document says that, while the US might benefit from these governments, the creation of a local anti-communist bloc would be more

7

trouble than its worth (page 11-12).

Another is document 6804033476, from the Intelligence section of the Defense Department, dated October 1 1976. Like all the rest, it worries that the militaries of the area aren't sharing much with the US about their operations, proving Condor was not a US project nor was it ever "American backed." Like most, it never mentions Marxism but thinks its an "anti-terrorist" movement. Like every other document in the Condor collection, it attacks the military governments at one level or anther and condemned their alleged human rights record, though mentions they're unsure of the nature of their sources.

Condor has long been a myth of the Left in the US, but like all of them, the internal documents, secret at the time, don't say what we're told they do. They demand the creation of liberal governments once terrorism has been stamped out and all seek to bring these governments "back into the US orbit," meaning that their counter-insurgency tactics must be less harsh. The US had nothing to do with these governments and never gave them aid of any kind. We're told "Condor" was an "American project," and yet, the US was largely kept in the dark about it. Frankly, it wasn't Washington's business.

Books on the subject, such as the ridiculous (2015) *History of Political Murder in Latin America: Killing the Messengers of Change* by John Green (SUNY Press) make reference to CIA involvement, but the documents don't say what he wants us to believe. Ultimately, these authors hope their readers don't actually read the documents themselves, and most certainly, they will not. Americans are told that the US "supported brutal dictators in Latin America" in the war against communism. Yet, these men weren't brutal and they never were backed by the US. Any "brutality" was easily matched by their enemies.

The sole concern of the US was the spread of terror tactics to the detriment of American citizens. Internal documents prove the US was against militarism in the area. More of these documents will be cited later saying the same thing. From this, I conclude that researchers in this field knowingly distort the written record to conform to the academic corporate culture. This is the polar opposite of what a scholar is meant to do.

Military governments existed to stop the country's slide into anarchy and economic depression. People weren't randomly killed. The Wikipedia article for "Operation

9

Condor" is a disgrace. Its Leftist propaganda that doesn't even pretend to be a descriptive, objective account. The very use of the phrase "death squad" shows the author to be either incompetent or dishonest. No such institutions existed. A "death squad" exists in every war. It's the function of an Army. What the article says – and all treatments of the subject say the same thing – and what the CIA or Defense Department say at the time are two different things. The policies of the US, as well as of the militaries of Latin America, aren't secret. Conformity is both easier and more professionally rewarding than actual scholarship or research.

Pinochet, for example, was not permitted to enter the US in the 1970s and Somoza's reelection bid in Nicaragua was condemned by both the American President and Congress. The US abandoned Batista early in the Cuban civil war. Batista, it might be noted, was the Communist candidate for president in 1940. Few realize that the Bacardi family, well known in the US among drinkers, backed Castro. Things are never what they seem. To picture a "spontaneous, heroic" Leftist rebellion and an oligarchy using the army to defend their ill-gotten gains is a monstrous distortion that never existed in Latin America.

As always, things are infinitely more complex. This paper will seek to make this infinity somewhat understandable.

This extended essay is a brief treatment of some of the more significant military dictatorships in Latin America. The point is to suggest that the assumptions and prejudices of almost every single journalist and academic in English are incorrect, sometimes deliberately so. A paper like this runs the risk of being too cursory when so much ground is being covered and so many errors exist that cry out for correction.

I'm very much aware that I'm leaving a lot out here, but that's the nature of the medium. If I've neglected to mention your favorite figure or event, you'll live. It might console the reader that the issue isn't so much policy detail, but rather proving that military rulers have generally been rational, determined, successful and strongly populist leaders thrust into the limelight during times of intense stress. Their policies generally worked in contrast to the democracies they supplanted.

The purpose of this paper is to be a counter-example to the litany of sins these military leaders allegedly committed. What I have here is a sample of what has been Left out of the mental universe of those writing on this subject today. No dictators murder for no reason, even Pol Pot saw himself as cleansing the country of social diseases. No one sees themselves as the bad guy. Given that, the historian's job isn't to pompously lecture the dead on their sins, but rather to understand these men in context. The worst part is that, if anyone can be accused of brutality as policy, it is exactly those the Anglo-American liberal establishment seek to defend: the Trotskys and Maos of the world. It is the Left, not the Right, that makes brutality a matter of not only state policy, but philosophical principle.

A word of caution: The armchair analyst, condescendingly shaking his head at my heresy – living in comfort and security – needs to remember the extreme tension, street violence, economic collapse, hyperinflation, drug addiction and polarization most of these countries suffered under at the time. These men need to be judged in this context, not whether or not it conforms to ideologies of the British Enlightenment or Marxist class analysis. Prejudices die hard, especially when hundreds of careers have been built on them.

The implication is that democratically elected leaders would not have done better and would likely have done much worse than the military. In fact, democracy's humiliating failures are precisely what caused these coups in the first place. Almost always, from Europe in the 1930s to Cold War South America, the pattern is that a legislative body comes to be made of politicians dependent on big money to function, creating deeply compromised elites and a profoundly divided legislature that cannot forcefully deal with national crises.

In all cases without exception, liberal democracies in the third world are paralyzed in the face of extreme violence, terrorism from all sides, consensus breakdown and, worst of all, the dominance of foreign money that uses their own weakness against them. Because of this, they are described in the pejorative, insulting term "banana republics." They more than earn it. No third world successes – not one – have occurred under liberalism. Of the several states that have become first world, clawing their way from poverty, all accomplished this largely under military or other authoritarian states: Park's Korea, theocratic Iran and Chang's Taiwan are the best known examples, but there are others.

Chapter 2.
Nicaragua

During the 1980s, aid to the "Contras" fighting the Marxist Sandinista government of Daniel Ortega in Nicaragua was an important foreign policy issue in the USA. It was assumed that Anastasio Somoza (1925-1980) was an evil man because he was a "military dictator." He ruled from 1967 to 1972 and again from 1974 to 1979. The truth is that he was a wise and popular ruler and far better for the country than any alternative. His main policy concern was to bring labor into national politics without Marxist violence. In fact, this is a common theme. This made him an obvious target for the Left because he was stealing their issues. He sinned against liberalism by refusing all foreign loans, seeking only local sources of funding. To believe that he was "supported" by Washington is a fantasy. He was overthrown by Washington working with the Sandinistas. Only the introduction of a strong Soviet presence later changed that.

Somoza preached that the oligarchs, men who neither trusted nor liked him, kept peasants ignorant. It has been repeated many times that he allegedly said "I don't want an educated population; I want oxen." This is assumed to be true without criticism. The truth is that this is what he said the communists wanted. It just so happens that this precise phrase, in translation, was used by Pol Pot in the mid 1970s in the "diagnosis" of "memory sickness." This is a historical reality made famous in the movie *The Killing Fields* of 1984. It is not fiction. "Memory sickness" was "thinking too much about life in pre-revolutionary Cambodia." Speaking of *Ankar*, or the party, the main character says they tell them "to be like the ox and have no thought, except for the party. . ."

Another myth is that he sold the blood, literally, of his population to blood banks in the US. One idiot even said, "Every morning the homeless, drunks, and poor people went to sell half a liter of blood for 35 (Nicaraguan) cordobas." No one bothered to tell this fool that drunks cannot donate blood. While he might have owned stock in such a business, its not inherently an evil field. It is, however, an easy business to make seem wicked in times of great economic stress.

It is even less known that regular elections were the norm under his rule. He was elected president in both 1967 and 1974. In the second election, out of 850,000 votes, he received roughly 700,000. The Organization of American

States oversaw the elections and dubbed them free and fair. At no time under either of his administrations were opposition newspapers shut down, though his successors rejected press freedom. Why a dictator wanting a population "like the oxen" would maintain elections and keep newspapers open is a question that has never been asked, let alone answered.

Ideologically, he was a Syndicalist and Corporatist. Most traditional Conservatives and Nationalists are in one form of another. He saw foreign industry as a great evil and a blight on the country. Most of all, he sought the redistribution of land to the peasants. Under his first administration, any land that could be farmed by anyone was theirs for the taking. Absentee landlords were proscribed. He also offered cheap credit and greatly curtailed usury, one of the perennial reasons the peasantry remained in debt and something curiously never mentioned by his Leftist opponents. At this time, he was considered a "socialist" by the US. This is why the State Department's Office for Latin America backed the FSLN for many years against Somoza, a fact never mentioned in the press at the time. Their leaders, Danny Ortega included, were feted by the elite in the US throughout the 1970s.

In his book *Nicaragua Betrayed,* entirely unread in English, he relates that in the 1960s, local politicians of all stripes, as well as judges were routinely murdered by communist death squads. A major source of funding for the Leninists in Central America was kidnapping children from prominent families and holding them for ransom. In El Salvador, President Duarte saw his daughter captured by the "heroic" FMLN and held for ransom. While Somoza could have destroyed the party at any time, he didn't, seeking an accommodation with them, since they allegedly agreed with him on land reform. They did not.

Somoza's book is worth reading. In 1976-1977, any aid to the army of Somoza was stopped. The ambassador from the US began talks with the Sandinistas. He relates that Robert Pastor, President Carter's personal representative, asked the president of Costa Rica rhetorically "When are we going to get that son of a bitch to the north out of the presidency?"

An accusation that is easy to verify and confirm is the fact that the State Department refused to accept clear proof that the Sandinista movement was backed by Cuba and therefore, the USSR. Soon afterwards, the IMF refused any credit for the country despite a solid economic performance under Somoza. It turns out the US pressured major banks to go elsewhere and ignore Nicaragua. The result was Somoza used other sources of credit to build a bunch of hydroelectric dams in the countryside. The US then threatened sanctions on those banks that had extended the credit.

If that wasn't sufficient, the US banned all coffee exports from the country as well as beef, an important sector of the economy. The US was planning on destroying the economy in order to unseat Somoza. Once the pressure worked and Somoza was unseated, one of the first things the Sandinistas did was to execute about 3,000 right wing politicians in the country, mostly local mayors and city councilmen. The Carter Administration gave special privileges for the USSR to use seaports close to Latin America in order to "trade" with the new government. Weapons were easily discernible in the cargo. All of this is from Chapter 20 of Somoza's book, but these are also very easy to confirm elsewhere. None of these were secret acts.

Somoza invited the hostile Human Rights Commission into the country, something Castro and others weren't known for doing. The Commission, which was financed by major banks and big foundations, assured

Somoza that it was a neutral commission. It was anything but. Somoza writes,

> The commission was caught in a quandary. What were they to do with those who came to testify [in favor of] the government? It didn't take them long to solve that dilemma. Their decision was shocking. They only wanted to hear those who had something to say against the government. To the chagrin of the Commission, numerous Nicaraguans went before that corrupt political entity to relate their misfortunes at the hands of the guerrillas. These people told of being shot, robbed, beaten, burned out, tortured, and witnessing murders. All crimes committed by the guerrillas. The commission turned a deaf ear. They wouldn't even listen and, furthermore, none of these heinous crimes were reported by a Commission charged with the responsibility of investigating human rights violations.

This is nothing new. What were the alternatives? For establishment academics and lawyers to admit that a military government was an excellent alternative to other forms? They would have been tarred immediately as "apologists" for "corrupt and brutal dictators." Their jobs would be in danger and they'd be subject to physical violence. The Commissions was highly significant, corrupt or no. From their Report, the US and other governments made their decision to destroy his government. This Report from the Commission was the foundation for all the stories, myths and lies about Somoza that are still being repeated today. It justified all their prejudices. Somoza relates, once in power, the Reds did the following:

> — The Sandinistas captured, tortured, and shot Lt. Juan Ocon. While he was still alive his head was cut off. His family could not find his head so the family buried him with a plaster head attached to the body.
> — Alvaro Sanchez was taken out of his home and shot in the presence of his mother and children.
> — Pedro Pablo Espinoza, newspaperman

and member of the Liberal Party, was captured by the Sandinistas in El Dorada. He was tortured, his eyes gouged out, and was then shot.

— In Leon, thirteen young members of the Guardia Nacional surrendered to the Sandinistas. They were taken to the football stadium in Leon where they were all shot.

— While Lt. Rene Silva, a member of the Guardia National from Matagalpa, was at the battle front, the Sandinistas went to him home and murdered his wife and two children, four and two years old.

— Dr. Rafael Saavedra, General Director of Customs, was burned alive by the Sandinistas and his two sons killed.

— Two female police students were captured. One of them was four months pregnant. They opened her up and pulled the fetus out. According to sworn testimony given to the U.S. House of Representatives and which appears in the February 26, 1980 Congressional Record, this group was under

the command of an American by the name
of Clifford Scott.

— Major Domingo Gutierrez and six of his
men were captured. They were placed in a
hole, sprayed with gasoline and burned
alive.

— Sergeant Edwin R. Ordonez of the
infantry training school was captured and
burned alive.

— Dr. Cornelio Hueck, former President of
the Congress, was captured at his ranch near
Rivas, He was taken to the town square of
Tola where he was shot several times in
non-vital areas. Then, with the people of the
town present, he was placed on a table and,
while he was still alive, his heart was cut
out.

— Major Pablo Emilio Salazar, better
known as "Comandante Bravo," was
captured by the Sandinistas in Honduras
after the war was over, and tortured to death.
His face was beaten beyond recognition, his
arms broken, his ears cut off, his genitals

severed, strips of his skin peeled from his body and, finally, he was shot in the head.

These are true because the exact same events occurred whenever a socialist government came to power. None of these acts were condemned by the US at the time and none were called the work of "death squads." In fact, while Somoza sent the US information like this, he received no reply. The person covering the war for *The New York Times,* Alan Riding, told Somoza to his face that he was both a socialist and sought the destruction of his government. However, it was Somoza that was accused of shutting down a free press.

He also related that it was the Jesuits of the Roman Church, not the communists, that were the most radical force in politics at the time. This was the same in El Salvador, where the FMLN got it start in the nominally Catholic universities. Unlike Eastern Europe, the church in Latin America, especially the Jesuit order that didn't have to listen to local bishops, was a critical pillar of the Marxist guerrilla forces. The Jesuits were solely answerable to Rome, not bishops. They were well-off, they ruled local universities and were the most radical elements of the

Roman church "reforming" itself in the 1960s in "Vatican Council II."

At no time in history did the United States support him and in fact, communications between Somoza and Washington were severed early on. Throwing western bankers out of your country generally doesn't make you popular in Washington. Selling weapons to a country isn't "support." *Giving* weapons to a country is. Trading openly with a country doesn't mean the trading partners are political allies. Trade isn't accomplished by governments anyway, but by profit-seeking private concerns. The US had a brisk trade in all sectors with the USSR without interruption from 1918 to 1990. When a journalist says "the US supported dictators!" he means no more than trade remained at the normal level. For them, "support" is anything short of harsh sanctions and a land invasion. Ultimately, thanks to both Soviet and American pressure, the only country willing to sell weapons to his army was Israel. While the Reagan administration supported the Contras with weapons, he did so while condemning Somoza in the harshest terms. He saw the Contras as representing the liberal alternative to the communists.

The CIA writes in their country description:

Although his [first] four-year term was to end in 1971, Anastasio Somoza Debayle amended the constitution to stay in power until 1972. Increasing pressures from the opposition and his own party, however, led the dictator to negotiate a political agreement, known as the Kupia-Kumi Pact, which installed a three-member junta that would rule from 1972 until 1974.

While this might be true, it neglects to mention that an earthquake tore the country apart in late 1972. More than anything else, this is the reason he needed to hang onto power and why so many reforms failed to materialize. Oddly, there were no gigantic rock concerts to assist the citizens of Nicaragua like Live Aid in 1985. Live aid, of course, was meant to send food aid to communist Ethiopia. When Lt. Col. Mengistu Miram was driven out of the Ethiopia in the early 1990s, I recall a comic of him running out of the country, followed by a hail of bullets. He's yelling back at his attackers saying, "that does it, no more Live Aid concerts!" It appears corporate America sees

25

some natural disasters as more important than others.

Anyway, the same source continues:

> The junta was established in May 1972
> amidst opposition led by Pedro Joaquin
> Chamorro Cardenal and his newspaper *La
> Prensa.* Popular discontent also grew in
> response to deteriorating social conditions.
> Illiteracy, malnourishment, inadequate
> health services, and lack of proper housing
> also ignited criticism from the Roman
> Catholic Church, led by Archbishop Miguel
> Obando y Bravo.

Still no mention of the earthquake that destroyed the capital. Even so, the economy of his era grew substantially. In 1974 alone, the GDP grew almost 14 percent, at least in part due to the government's reconstruction effort after the quake. The CIA dismiss his economic success as "merely a reflection of the high world prices for coffee and cotton." In other words, his economic success was an accident. If the mere possession of high demand resources led to such growth, then why aren't diamond-rich African states experiencing the same growth? Why isn't oil-rich Chad a dominant regional power? Or Somalia for that matter?

As it turns out, growth from 1961 to 1980 is far greater than from 1990 to 2003, even without taking the earthquake into consideration. Gross capital formation soared under Somoza. While early in his government, he ran a trade surplus, that slowly went away as the economy recovered and imports increased. Significantly, external debt was non-existent under Somoza. From 1980 to 1994, it went from almost zero to 1200 percent of GNI. At no point was substantial land reform accomplished except under Somoza (all the above statistics are from *World Development Indicators 2005,* World Bank). In El Salvador, even at the height of the civil war, economic growth was slight, but very real.

Eventually, the CIA's description mentions the quake, which killed 10,000 people and wounded 40,000 at a minimum. About 90 percent of city housing in Managua was left unstable. They say "Government budget deficits and inflation were the legacies of the earthquake." Yet even his attempt to rebuild the country is spun as a negative. "The government increased expenses to finance rebuilding, which primarily benefited the construction industry, in

27

which the Somoza family had strong financial interests." If he refuses to assist, he's a monster. If he does, he's a monster. If he gives a dollar to charity, its to make him popular with others. If he doesn't, he's just greedy. The man can't win, but such writing is the opposite of journalism or scholarship.

Unfortunately, the quake forced the government to borrow from abroad. The elites in the city of Leon controlled the banking of the country, shifted to the US under the Sandinistas. Few guerrillas make good bankers. This was done in the face of American "sanctions" against the Sandinistas, though such sanctions were against only a few agricultural products. The elite of the country's second largest city were on the Left of the political spectrum, as many bankers are. In no way were the country's financial elites pro-Somoza or even pro-Contra.

Once the civil war was sparked by Cuba with American support, the "accidental" economic growth "ground" to a halt despite coffee prices remaining fairly high. Under the Sandinista regime, economic growth remained flat, inflation soared and, contrary to all promises, only about ten percent of capital was nationalized. The military in El Salvador, for example, nationalized far more than that before 1984.

During the fierce debates in the US in the 1980s, the assumptions about Somoza's government were false. American conservatives fell all over themselves trying to argue that the Contras were not formerly part of his National Guard, as if any connection to him was political death. He was assassinated in exile, with Castro taking the credit. As a comical aside, the Wikipedia page for him states, "In 1979, the Brazilian newspaper *Gazeta Mercantil* estimated that the Somoza family's fortune amounted to between $2 billion and $4 billion with its head, Anastasio Somoza Debayle, owning $1 billion." Looking at the footnote, that's not the newspaper at all, but rather the *World Marxist Review,* Volume 22. Why would the authors mention the Brazilian newspaper in the article only to cite the Marxist paper in the footnotes?

That figure has been cited in many works on the subject without the slightest criticism. How could the communist paper know this? If the figure came from Ortega's government, then it should be doubted. At least, they should have inquired equally into his own personal fortune. Leon Trotsky for example, at the time of his axing, was worth between $1 billion and $4 billion, depending on the source. Otherwise, did these journalists break into the presidential palace and steal Somoza's ledgers? If he were so wealthy, why, when his government was militarily in trouble, didn't he hire new soldiers or mercenaries? With such money, how was he assassinated with such ease? Wouldn't he have been able to afford a substantial personal militia? I don't know the answer to these questions, but I also wasn't a journalist in the 1980s.

Chapter 3.
Peru

In Peru, General Juan Velasco took over the country because the democratically elected government, especially President Fernando Belaunde was going to give her oil fields to American investors. The army took these immensely strategic resources under its control. Velasco is one of the most articulate, successful and firmly nationalist military leaders in history. Because of this, he's rarely treated to the same invective given to other military leaders in this era. His government lasted from 1968 to 1975 and it was the most successful economic era in Peruvian history.

Velasco was a former shoe-shine boy in Pilura. His parents had 11 children and lived in poverty. Needless to say, Belaunde came from one of the most elite families in the country. His father served as the finance minister to President Jose Bustamonte, who ended his career at the International Court at the Hague. The whole family was educated in the US. The formerly poverty-stricken Velasco relished overthrowing the arrogant Belaunde regime. The former worked his way up the military ladder, the other received his riches from his family.

The coup leaders in Peru named their administration

the "Revolutionary Government of the Armed Forces," with Velasco at its helm as President. Velasco's administration articulated a desire to assist Peru's poorest people through a policy of nationalization known as *Peruanismo*. Velasco's rule was characterized by policies which aimed to create a strong national industry to increase the international independence of Peru. This is a classic nationalist concern. He nationalized entire industries, expropriated many corporations from fisheries to mining to telecommunications to power production and consolidated them into single conglomerates on the South Korean model. These government-run entities included *PescaPeru, MineroPeru, Petroperú, SiderPeru,Centromin Peru, ElectroPeru, Enapu, EnatruPeru, Enafer, Compañia Peruana de Telefonos, EntelPeru, Correos del Peru* and many others. He passed a law saying that any foreign firm in Peru prior to 1971 had to become half Peruvian in five years.

Importantly, his first order of business was to nationalize the central bank. This was his first act, writing the decree on December 31, 1968, Decree Law 17330 was issued. The main provision was that 75 percent of all owners had to be native Peruvians and they could not be part of the old oligarchy.

These were meant to discourage private investment in those sectors, keeping the economy under state control and away from the reach of western capital. There is nothing remarkable in this since these goals were identical to almost all Latin American coups of the era. This is so similar to General Park's agenda in South Korea that a connection must be present.

Most reforms were planned by nationalist intellectuals and most were successful in that they improved the Peruvian quality of life. The prejudice in academia is that the Right is "pro-capitalist." This is false. The Right is broadly syndicalist and Hegelian, but accepting of limited private property. The "unlimited" right to property has never been a Rightist position anywhere. While it is true that, in the Cold War era, "conservatism" became vaguely associated with libertarianism, the truth is that the two ideologies are almost total opposites elsewhere. "Free market capitalism" is a revolutionary, materialist and modernist ideology.

Velasco was no less nationalist than his colleagues in other Latin American militaries. All of these military leaders sought to nationalize certain properties if they could, or least ensure that locals alone could invest in strategic sectors. Velasco, like all the rest, sought a radical reform of education that stressed national identity. The Peruvian education reform of 1972 provided for bilingual instruction for the local Indian population of the Andes and the Amazon, which was almost half of the population in the 1970s. In 1975, the Velasco government decreed that Quechua was one of the official languages of Peru, equal to Spanish. Thus, Peru was the first Latin American country to make an indigenous language equal to the dominant Spanish or Portuguese.

Peruanismo required long term planning. The short-term mentality is one of the weaker elements of liberal systems. The rotation of politicians makes long term planning almost impossible. At a minimum, it encourages a professional bureaucracy that is impervious to short term changes in political dominance. Bureaucracies are identical to one another regardless of the nature of the political system. State newspapers were founded to compete with the often foreign-owned local dailies. These reforms are consistently nationalist and they worked.

A foundational part of Velasco's economic scheme was an agrarian reform program to expropriate large landowners to diversify land ownership. There is not a single military government in Latin America that did not try to do this at one level or another. In its first ten years in power, the Revolutionary Government expropriated 15,000 plots totaling 22 million acres and benefited some 300,000 families. Only a military government can do this since it alone has the power to go over the heads of the elite. To this day, academics and journalists have refused to accept this obvious fact of life. This is also part of the reason why soldiers are often popular politicians.

In his *First Principles,* Velasco wrote that the purpose of his reform was

(a) to regulate and limit the right to land ownership in harmony with the social interest; (b) to redistribute the land to small and medium size proprietors who work it themselves; (c) to guarantee communal rights of ownership of the farming communities … (d) to organize and regulate cooperatives for exploiting the land; (e) to regulate agrarian contracts and to eliminate indirect forms of exploitation in order that the land may belong o those who work it; (f) to regulate rural labor and social security, abolishing any relationship between granting use of the land and the rendering of personal services; and (g) to promote agricultural and livestock development (Quoted from Alxander, 2007: 92).

The former landlords who opposed this argued that their compensation was poor and that the peasants lacked the skill to manage properties themselves. They were paid in agrarian reform bonds, which turned out to be meaningless paper when the government began to suffer from high inflation. Peru has the lowest amount of arable land per capita in South America. Less than two percent of the Peruvian territory is arable, with 98 percent composed of arid desert with little rain, harsh mountains and very steep terrain.

Given this, Velasco's system was successful and necessary. Democratic politicians had failed miserably to reform social life given the fact that they were dependent on wealthy – often foreign – supporters to finance expensive campaigns. With few other organized, educated and patriotic groups in existence, the army was forced to take matters into their own hands. Their record is an excellent one.

Of all the Spanish speaking military leaders of his era, he maintained the most substantial and interesting ideological approach to political rule. Both land redistribution and oil nationalization were his greatest successes and kept production in Peruvian hands. Steel and iron, which became significant parts of the economy under his control, were maintained in state hands despite threats from the US. Limiting elite land-ownership led to his being called a "communist" in Washington.

His "Industrial Communities" were profit sharing associations unique to Peru. Labor became institutionally part of management, ownership and profits. Regardless of other factors, 15 percent of all pre-tax income went to local needs. Labor was guaranteed a full 50 percent of ownership in all state and private bodies of any size. They've been described like this:

> Under this law, an "industrial community"
> was established in an enterprise by the
> Ministry of Industry and Trade at the request

of any worker. All permanent employees—those who had successfully passed the three-month probationary period and worked at least a four-hour day—constituted an industrial community and were entitled to share in its management, profit ts and ownership. Membership was limited to one community per individual.

Industries were compelled to distribute 25 percent of their pretax income in the following manner: 15 percent for the "industrial community" (comprising all the workers of any firm having more than six workers) in the form of equity in the enterprise (some communities were permitted to purchase up to 50 percent ownership in the firm) and 10 percent in cash to individuals workers. Worker participation in essential industries, however, was subject to the state's discretion. Under the law, a worker with veto rights had to be a member of the board of directors (Quoted from Alexander, 94).

These were meant to be "self management" organizations based vaguely on the Yugoslav model. Owners were very upset and sought to sabotage these reforms. They refused to permit meetings, insisted on using English, lied about profits and went to the US for assistance. The Left, seeing their issues taken away, claimed that "these [communities] are a means of destroying labor unions." They certainly were. They were no longer unions as they became institutionalized as part of the legal structure of the country.

One of his essential successes is to reduce the country's reliance on foreign investment. There's no military government in Latin history that didn't have this as part of its agenda. In 1968, 35 percent of all capital in Peru was owned by foreigners, by the time he left office, it was 17 percent despite huge economic growth He built a large domestic market at the same time. There's a very good reason he's not often discussed in university classrooms.

Velasco knew that a revolution cannot just come from the top. This was an error of the Leninists that Marx instituted explicitly during the First International. He needed a literate, civic-minded population. In 1971,

Velasco created the *Sistema Nacional de Apoyo a la Movilizacion Social* (or the National System of Support of Social Mobilization—SINAMOS). General Leonidas Rodriguez was its head, but civilians had a strong role in it too. It consolidated ten sectors of the state. This was no political party, but an attempt at mass education. The law establishment this said its purpose was:

> 1. Training, orientation and organization of the national population.
> 2. Development of entities of social interest.
> 3. Communications
> and particularly
> 4. To [promote] the the dialogue between the Government and the national population."
> Further, it would "foster labor unions" when necessary (Quoted from Alexander, 95).

Since the court system had long since been a bastion of the old oligarchs, the military alone had the power to overthrow them. He replaced them with a new, independent system based on American models called the Courts of the Land. No judge was permitted to own land or any

40

substantial amount of capital. Along with the industrial communes, he also founded agricultural cooperatives where usury was banned and the court system was internal. He broke the old oligarchy. He actually did what the Left just promised. By 1975, almost 65 percent of land was in peasant hands. Oddly, this coincided with the intensification of Leftist agitation in the countryside. Without it, it would have been 100 percent.

His main support base was both the industrial proletariat as well as the peasantry. Long abandoning the urban population to the military, the Left went to Maoist terror rather than attempting to compete with Velasco, forcing the guerrilla Shining Path organization to rely on terror. The alternative Tupac Amaru Revolutionary Movement was at one point run by a Jewish female university professor from Long Island named Lori Berenson, who was left alive after capture since she was also Israeli Mossad. This was the "representative" nature of the guerrillas. The substantial gains of the military government forced Shining Path to pure terrorism, including the Lucanamarca massacre of peasants in 1983.

The tragicomic affair of the vile Berenson was based around the plot of the MRTA to take members of the legislature hostage. This is the same outfit that in December 1996 stormed the Japanese ambassador's residence in Lima, holding 72 hostages for more than four months. Two soldiers and one hostage died in an otherwise successful rescue mission.

During her trial, the judge and jurors were forced to wear hoods lest they be targets of Leftist fighters. She actually screamed her guilt in court, yelling in her Yiddish accent, "There are no criminal terrorists in the MRTA! It is a revolutionary movement!" Explaining her outburst, her parents, powerful Mossad members in New York, claimed she, on her way to court, passed a cell where cops were torturing a man. Thus, she was hysterical. No one knows how her parents a) were relevant to anything, b) knew this impressive bit of datum or c) how she even got a trial. Would her opponents ever get a trial? When a terrorist is on trial, do his parents usually get to weigh in on the matter? Well, she's no ordinary terrorist.

Like in so many other places, these terror cells had rendered the justice system nearly on the verge of collapse, hence the hoods. Judges who tried and convicted terrorists were hounded and murdered. Witnesses who gave evidence met a similar fate. Not only did the supply of witnesses dry up, the number of judges willing to risk their lives shrank almost to nothing. If the state had not extended to judges and witnesses the protection of anonymity, there would have been no trials of terrorists at all in Peru. Society would have collapsed, which was one of the central aims of people like Berenson. She never denied her role in the attack, so the notion of a "trial" made no sense except to determine her fate. At the same time, usually, members of such organizations are shot during the commission of the crimes. Someone was tipped off that she was Mossad and part of a very powerful New York clique.

Berenson's lawyers, including the appalling Ramsey Clark, the former U.S. attorney general made the silly argument that the hoods rendered her trial illegitimate, despite it being forced by the Leftists themselves. The only real consolation here is that Berenson exposed the strong Mossad and general Jewish role in Leftist terror in Peru *The Wall Street Journal,* hardly an anti-Jewish institution, wrote:

> No wonder that the Peruvian people have no sympathy for Berenson. She had little local public support at the time of her conviction.

43

Even today, after years in jail, she has more support on the Upper West Side of Manhattan than she does in all Lima. In a poll conducted recently by El Comercio, a Lima newspaper, 52% of those questioned said they disapproved of her getting a new trial. A third of all respondents felt that her retrial was the outcome not of new evidence, nor of a flawed first trial, but of plain, old-fashioned American pressure.

"American" pressure? Really? Since when does the US government go out of their way to demand the proper treatment of Maoist terrorists? When they're Jewish, that's when. While the author of the WSJ editorial was strictly forbidden to mention her ethnicity (though his "Lower East Side" comment was meant to give the clear implication), the basis of the "concern" is clear. If it were anyone else, she would have been shot long ago. As it turns out, many politicians such as Jesse Jackson and the Clinton State Department, at the time run by the Jewish Madeline Albright, claimed she was a mere "human rights activist." Recently, and inexplicably, she's been released and sent to

Israel, a place she's never been. She got away with dozens of murders.

Peasants, hating the Left, organized their own military forces. Local peasant militias, vehemently against the Shining Path, captured and killed their local commander Olegario Curitomay. The Shining Path got revenge by killing 69 peasants, 18 of whom were children. They did it again in Marcas, during August of 1985. Just before that, the Path killed 47 peasants in Hauyllo, 17 of whom were under 15. Peasant militia forces, called "*rondas*," came into existence largely because of the popularity of Velasco's government. Having seen many of their demands long accomplished through him, the Path had little purpose.

Since the Shining Path deliberately do not wear uniforms, no "human rights abuses" can be committed against them. According to international law, all guerrilla groups must show some sort of identifying mark that can be seen from a distance, which is usually a uniform of some kind. If a civilian is killed in the mistaken impression he's a terrorist, then the Path is responsible, not the army. Therefore, any reference to "human rights" relative to attacks on the Maoists by definition must be false.

Due to their lack of support, the Shining Path forcibly recruited young men by "conscription." Most of the group's activities were setting off bombs in market squares and generally targeting civilian populations. Oddly, the calling card of the MRTA is the hanging of dogs and cats from lampposts before an attack would begin – or after, depending on circumstances, I guess. Peruvians of all political stripes hate this Jewish woman and, in general, most of the Maoist terrorist cells. The reason that Peru will never fall to the Jewish professor-types is General Velasco, one of the greatest leaders in Latin American history. As might be expected, his 1975 removal from power soon led to the old oligarchy regaining their position in the country.

Unfortunately, the mid 1970s were a tough time for world markets. Inflation grew in Peru and the state was forced to borrow abroad. This means foreign banks had a say in domestic politics, the last thing Velasco wanted. The Left pretended this was the fault of the "reactionary regime" and sought to bring it down. Communist labor unions, especially the CGPT, engaged in many strikes in order to destroy the implementation of Velasco's reforms. As always, private capital and the communists worked together in favor of free trade and the destruction of the

Velasco government. It's worth noting that in every communist country in existence, organized labor was banned outright.

Because of all this, his revolution wasn't given the time it needed to develop. A young Hugo Chavez visited Peru before Velasco's death and was given a copy of his *The Peruvian Revolution.* Chavez said he read the book many times and sought to bring some of its insights into Venezuela. He ordered its reprinting in millions of copies when he took over.

Velasco became ill, seriously so, and he lost a leg to an embolism a year before he was voted out by the junta in 1975. That very day, Velasco addressed the nation and said he "would not do battle with the military" seeking to overthrow him on the grounds that "Peruvians should not be fighting one another." He died two years later, his casket being carried around Lima for two hours while crowds thronged the procession, throwing flowers.

Chapter 4.
Colombia

In Columbia, civil unrest, political upheaval and public discontent had turned the country into a war zone. Angry and violent street demonstrations and a general strike in May 1957 brought down the government of General Gustavo Rojas Pinilla. At the age of 47, General Paris Gordillo was selected by Rojas to act as a caretaker government from 1957 to 1958. General Gordillo assumed the Presidency with two other generals, Luis Castillo and Rafael Pardo, a general from the National Police Service. General Gordillo was elected as chairman of the junta, and as such, became chief executive.

It should be noted that Rojas was also an accomplished civil servant. He passed the law that, for better or worse, gave women the ability to vote. While of dubious value, he introduced the television and constructed several hospitals, universities and the National Astronomic Observatory. Public works was his main focus, and this didn't change later. He financed projects such as the Atlantic railway, the hydroelectric dam of Lebrija, and the oil refinery of Barrancabermeja.

The first decrees of the junta were aimed to restore

peace and order, freedom of speech and association, freedom of the press, adherence to the Constitution and calling for a presidential election as soon as possible. The democratic government failed to do this because of its weakness and division. Its inaction and incompetence destroyed its legitimacy.

In order to ease tensions, the junta also appointed cabinet ministers the leaders of both major political parties. Unlike the banana republic they replaced, they forced a consensus on Columbia while liberalism created greater division to the point of blood. The violence between the two political parties decreased first when Gustavo Rojas, one of Gordillo's predecessors, deposed the reigning president of Colombia. Since the country was seemingly losing a war with communist forces, he quickly negotiated with the guerrillas, seeking at least a temporary peace to begin reconstruction.

After Rojas' own deposition, the Colombian Conservative Party and the Colombian Liberal Party agreed to create the National Front, a coalition which would jointly govern the country. Under the deal, the presidency would alternate between conservatives and liberals every 4 years for 16 years; the two parties would have parity in all other elective offices. The National Front ended *"La Violencia,"* and National Front administrations attempted to institute far-reaching social and economic reforms.

"La Violencia" proved the nature of liberal democracy to Colombia. Both major parties had their own militaries that fought it out in the 1950s. It destroyed the economy and caused most to reject the absurd assumptions of democratic thinking. The press, afraid of revenge attacks, refused to report on many of the battles. There was no order, so the court system failed. Elections, in other words, was an excuse for more violence.

The coup against Rojas was accepted in the December 1 referendum. The military had to run the country otherwise, or no election, of any kind, would have occurred. For the National Front, each party was to present lists of nominees to compete in a sort of "primary system." The National Front established rules to run within parties and preserve in some way the democratic system.

The Conservative Party could not reach an agreement on who would be its first candidate to govern, and after consulting with the Liberal Party, both sides agreed to start with a Liberal candidate. A constitutional amendment was passed which also extended the National

Front from 12 to 16 years. In 1958 elections for the presidency were reestablished, and on May 4, as expected Alberto Lleras Camargo is elected the first president of the National Front.

The National Front gradually pacified the bipartisan violence that endured for more than a century and allowed the demobilization of some liberal guerrillas. However, social, economic and political problems continued and new guerrilla movements grew due to the general dissatisfaction. In 1964 the Revolutionary Armed Forces of Colombia (FARC) guerrilla group was born and was followed by other groups such as the National Liberation Army (ELN) on January 7, 1965, the Popular Liberation Army (EPL) on July 1967, the Quintín Lame Movement (MAQL) in 1984 and the 19th of April Movement (M-19). Almost all had foreign backing.

Besides restoring peace, the junta's other concern was the economy. The state had a huge deficit, a large trade deficit and overall, the national debt was over $500 million. Again, liberalism the world over has failed to address these issues, especially in the third world. The problems facing these poor states cannot be adequately addressed by politicians reliant on a small clique of elites for funding and direction. This situation caused very high unemployment and triggered an economic depression.

In order to address this, the junta created an economic and financial task force, presided over by Alfonso Pumarejo and Mariano Perez who were promptly sent to the United States to secure an emergency loan of $100 million to stimulate the economy, pay some foreign debt and invigorate employment. It was only the law and order imposed by the army that made this possible. This mission was also to negotiate a price agreement for coffee, essential to the economic health of Colombia. The commission also promoted technical educational and created the *"Servicio Nacional de Aprendizaje"* (SENA). Here again, the military did what liberalism either would not or could not do.

Regarding international trade and commerce, the administration of General Gordillo and the junta implemented the *Plan Vallejo,* designed to promote and stimulate exports and to reduce unnecessary imports easily produced at home. As always, this is the opposite of neoliberalism and led to predictable condemnations by the United States. The junta also encouraged foreign private investment and eased monetary policy and its accompanying exchange rates. General Gordillo initiated international negotiations with major economic powers to establish what would be known as the *"Pacto Mundial"* or the "World Accord." Once done, the junta would call a general election.

Despite some progress, guerrilla groups were created with foreign money (as well as the drug trade) such as the FARC, the ELN and the M-19 to fight the government. The coalition idea is far superior to anything that a liberal state would have or could have done given the emergency situation the country was facing. The guerrillas were threatened, not by violence, but by the rise of populist generals that were stealing their agenda and actually implementing some of their demands.

Since the 1960s, as is well known, Colombia has been damaged severely from a drawn-out war of attrition between government and Leftist guerrilla groups. The conflict escalated in the 1990s, but several guerrilla organizations decided to demobilize after peace negotiations developed between 1989–1994. The United States has been involved in the conflict since its beginnings, when in the early 1960s, the US government helped supply the Colombian military. Contrary to liberal mythology, American companies like Chiquita fruit feared military rule since they feared nationalization and profit sharing, a common demand of the armies of Latin America. American capital demands weak, divided, liberal states they can easily control. It is absurd to think that they would support a populist general like Velasco or Gordillo.

The expansion of the coffee industry laid the groundwork for national economic integration after World War II. During the course of the postwar expansion, Colombia's economy grew tremendously. Before the 1950s, because of the steep terrain and a primitive transportation network, an oligarchy developed. This meant that capital investment required greater economic integration that could be provided only by very large corporations. Only a handful of firms could integrate the sector under those conditions.

Improved transportation facilities, financed directly and indirectly by the coffee industry, fostered national development. Greater economic integration soon became a reality with the more substantial concentration of industry. Coffee's success, therefore, led ultimately to a reliable transportation network that hastened urbanization and industrialization. In this case, the private-sector/military alliance built the country with a relatively high rate of success. All the while, the Left sought to cripple this expansion and growth. This fact was the cause of military governments.

In addition to coffee production, the expansion of both the industrial and the service sector took place in two clear stages. From 1950 until 1967, Colombia's military followed a well-defined program of import-substitution, with most manufacturing startups directed toward domestic consumption. Before then, of course, it had been satisfied by imports. Almost all military governments angered the US with these programs. After 1967, planners in both government and industry shifted the economic strategy to export promotion, emphasizing more diverse exports such as clothing and other manufactured consumables, in addition to processed coffee.

Thanks to military rule, Columbia was headed to first world status. Under a democracy, dependency would have been far greater as a small political elite, tied to coffee, would be making the decisions. The military was the only body that could serve as a counterweight to the communists, drug dealers and the economic elite. In Colombia, despite its struggles, democracy means utter disintegration.

Chapter 5.
Bolivia

The history of Bolivia from 1964 to 1982 is a time of periodic instability under various military dictators. In November 1964 the elected president, Víctor Paz Estenssoro, was overthrown by a military junta under vice-president General Rene Barrientos. Barrientos was elected in 1966, but died in a helicopter crash three years later, leading to a coup in September by General Ovando, who was in turn overthrown in October 1970 by General Rogelio Miranda who was, yet again, overthrown a couple of days later by General JJ Torres, who in turn was overthrown on August 1971 by Hugo Banzer Suarez. This chaos was only brought to an end under Banzer.

Banzer ruled for seven years, initially from 1971 to 1974 with the support of Estenssoro's Nationalist Revolutionary Movement. In 1974, impatient with schisms in the party, he replaced civilians with members of the armed forces and suspended political activities. The economy grew impressively during Banzer's presidency, but demands for greater political freedom undercut his support. This is as typical as it is ironic. The middle class created by military governments seeks more power

57

corresponding with their incomes. This has nothing to do with abstract democracy but derives from the desire of the newly empowered middle classes to buy their way into power. They turn on the government that created them.

In 1978 Bolivia once again was plunged into turmoil. Juan Pereda ruled only four months that year, but his ascent to the presidency marked the beginning of an even more unstable period in Bolivian history, with nine civilian and military presidents in little over four years (1978–1982). 1982 marked the return to a democratically elected government, with Guido Vildoso as president. Economic growth ground to a halt.

On November 4, 1964 Rene Barrientos Ortuno (president, 1964–69) and General Alfredo Ovando Candia declared themselves co-presidents. But as the crowd, which had gathered outside the palace, persisted in shouting its preference for the more charismatic Barrientos, Ovando allowed Barrientos to assume the formal title alone, while he occupied the post of commander in chief of the armed forces. This, we suppose, is direct democracy in action.

Barrientos is an excellent case study because he ruled both as a military man and as an elected politician. The difference was night and day, a fact that strongly supports the argument of this paper. He insisted that his assumption of power was not a counterrevolutionary move and promised to restore the Bolivian National Revolution to its "true path" from which the Movement had deviated during these twelve-years of instability.

His government continued many of the policies of the second Víctor Paz Estenssoro administration, including the acceptance of the International Monetary Fund (IMF) stabilization plan and the Triangular Plan. With this, the whole purpose of a military government was denied. Military states seek independence from these bodies, not guidance from them. Only the military has the strength to do this and it is the foundation of their legitimacy.

For the army to do what any democratic legislature would do removes the credibility of the military ruler. In this case, the emphasis on reducing social spending damaged the army's position. In May 1965, the army forced Barrientos to accept Ovando as his co-president as a reward for suppressing an uprising by miners and factory workers upset with IMF demands and the reduction of social spending.

The economy improved during the Barrientos regime at a rate averaging 6.5 percent per year. This was not to be again seen in that country's history. The rise of tin prices resulted in the growth of the state owned Mining Corporation of Bolivia *(Corporación Minera de Bolivia, Comibol)* and in 1966 contributed to the increased production in the medium-sized mines that had remained in private hands. Barrientos encouraged the private sector and foreign investment and gave the Gulf Oil Company permission to export petroleum and natural gas from Bolivia. Again, this removes the whole purpose for such a government. The state was losing all independence and freedom of action.

In 1966 Barrientos won an election through his Popular Christian Movement *(Movimiento Popular Cristiano, MPC)* as his base of support. Although the MPC was not very successful, he won the election with a coalition of conservative politicians and the peasantry. Barrientos's efforts to build support in the countryside succeeded at first with the signing in February 1964 of the Military-Peasant Pact *(Pacto Militar-Campesino)*. Under the agreement, the *campesino* militias agreed to adopt an anti-Leftist stance and to subordinate themselves to the army. His attempt to impose taxes on peasants, on the other hand, resulted in a vehement rejection. Had he maintained the import substitution of other military governments, this would probably not have become a necessity.

Still in thrall to the IMF, Barrientos took away most of the gains labor had achieved during the MNR's rule. He placed *Comibol* under the control of a military director and abolished the veto power of union leaders in management decisions. He also cut the pay of the miners and reduced the mining work force and the enormous *Comibol* bureaucracy by 10 percent. Finally, he destroyed the Bolivian Labor Federation *(Central Obrera Boliviana, COB)* and the mine workers' union, suppressed all strike activity, disarmed the miners' militias and exiled union leaders. Keep in mind that this was done at the insistence of the IMF and only after he became an "elected" politician. This cannot be a coincidence. Once he won an election, it was like he became a different person. In the third world, democracy destroys nations

Barrientos could not completely silence the labor sector as miners led the growing opposition to his rule and the unpopularity of neoliberalism, which always has to be maintained by force. The various opposition groups opposing this joined in denouncing Barrientos's selling of natural resources to the United States. They resented his invitation for Americans to invest in Bolivia because he offered greater privileges to foreign investors. These "non-discrimination" laws were also forced on the country by the IMF. The defection of Barrientos's close friend and minister of interior, Colonel Antonio Arguedas, to Cuba after his announcement that he had been an agent for the United States Central Intelligence Agency (CIA) aroused national indignation. Here, a former soldier turned "democrat" had given the country over to the US and the IMF. This is exactly why previous military governments existed to fight. How this can be laid at the feet of the army or "right wing" politics exists only in the liberal imagination.

The death of Barrientos in a helicopter crash on April 27, 1969 initially left control in the hands of his vice president, Luis Salinas. Real power, however, remained with the armed forces under its commander in chief, General Ovando, who took power on September 26, 1969 in a coup that was supported by reformist officers.

Ovando (co-president, May 1965 – January 1966, and president, January–August 1966 and 1969–1970) annulled the elections scheduled for 1970, dismissed the Congress and appointed a cabinet that included those who

had opposed the policies of Barrientos. Elections would
have led to chaos given the mood of the population.
Ovando hoped to gain civilian and military support with a
program of revolutionary nationalism, which he had
outlined in the *Revolutionary Mandate of the Armed
Forces.*

Revolutionary nationalism reflected the heritage and
rhetoric of the military reformist regimes of the past, as
well as the spirit of the 1952 Revolution. It also showed the
influence of the Peruvian government of Gen. Velasco.
Many Bolivian officers believed that the military had to
intervene in politics because civilian governments had
failed to stand up to the IMF. The policies of that
consortium of bankers are almost always a disaster since
they reflect the interest of the foreign elites that control
credit. The army would explicitly fight against social
injustice and economic dependence, true to their own roots
among the poor. This has been the sole purpose of military
governments and their sole source of legitimacy. The
moment they fail to do this, their legitimacy is gone.

The army nationalized the local assets of the Gulf
Oil Company. The Sandinistas wouldn't even take
measures of this kind. Ovando failed to gain popular

support due to the legacy of his "elected" predecessor, but once the army ruled on its own, it nationalized major western firms and plowed this cash into public works. Elections mean dependency on big money, especially foreign money. Militaries usually don't require such support. The claim that the United States "supported military dictators" is absurd at numerous levels, the economic is just one. The US, with a limited ideological vocabulary, referred to him as a "communist." Thinking that any non- or anti-capitalist measure is "Marxist" is typical of the American ignoramus, but it had painfully seeped into the highest levels of foreign policy-making. The poverty of the third world is the result.

Popular enthusiasm in Bolivia over the nationalization was short lived. Disagreement over compensation, a boycott of Bolivian crude oil on the international market and a general downturn in the economy became critical problems. Even though Ovando legalized the COB and withdrew troops from the mining camps, labor still did not trust the state. Frustrated expectations, broken promises, and the massacre of miners by the military in Catavi in 1967 had radicalized the workers who now refused to cooperate with the military they once saw as their salvation. Their view is understandable, but erroneous. The truth is that it wasn't the army, but elected leaders following elite, IMF dictates, that caused these events and created the resultant contempt. Without the need for foreign money to run a campaign, the army was more free than any politician, but labor was being influenced by Cuban and other forces that were threatened by true populism. Worse, army policy was inconsistent and Ovando himself was indecisive.

While labor became radicalized, the local capitalists became weary of Ovando's vacillating statements, which included the suggestion that private property be abolished. Even when Ovando moved to the "Right" during the last months of his regime, he was unable to enlist the support of the conservative groups because this repeated change only emphasized his weakness. In other words, he began to behave like a typical banana republic democrat

Ovando's reform program also polarized the military. Reformist officers, concerned about the decline in popular support for the army since Barrientos decided to become a politician, shifted their backing to the more radical General Juan Jose Torres Gonzalez, while others backed General Rogelio Miranda. One of the great problems plaguing western academics and journalists is that they want easy labels to pin on the men they cover. These labels go far in altering how the public might see a government figure and they're almost always misleading.

The problem is that American labels are idiosyncratic, not easily applicable to foreign states. The "conservative versus libertarian" problem was mentioned above. While capitalism is a "conservative" position in the postwar US, it has never been in the lexicon of conservative thought elsewhere. Terms like "liberal" or "reformer" are literally meaningless and can be stretched to cover almost any set of policies. All the generals mentioned in this paper were socially conservative. There are no exceptions to this. What differed were their views on the market and general economic policy.

The chaos surrounding the overthrow of Ovando highlighted the division in the armed forces. Military officers demanded the resignation of Ovando and Miranda after a failed coup attempt by the latter on October 5, 1970. A triumvirate, formed on October 6, failed to create confidence. On October 7, as the country moved toward civil war after the COB had declared a general strike and General Torres emerged as the compromise candidate and became president.

The main feature of Torres's presidency was a lack of decisiveness. Rather than taking the initiative on policies, Torres primarily reacted to political pressure. Again, he behaved more like an elected politician than a military leader. He was destroying the whole reason for a military junta. He nationalized even more American property, such as the waste-processing operation of the Catavi tin mines and the Matilde zinc mine, and he ordered the Peace Corps, considered a CIA front, out of the country.

While limiting American influence, Torres increased cooperation with the Soviet Union and its allies in the economic and technical sectors. Yet the American Left sees him as a "right wing" dictator. Still, even a "right wing dictator" can approach the USSR if there are no other options. This fact in itself isn't indicative of a leader's ideology. Saddam Hussein in Iraq and Hafez al-Assad in Syria were both Soviet clients without being communists.

Because of his lack of a clear strategy and political experience, Torres soon alienated all sectors of Bolivian society. He found it very difficult to organize socialist groups because they confronted him with demands that he could not meet, such as giving them half of all cabinet seats. Is this democratic? The workers, students, and parties of the Left wanted a socialist state and saw the Torres government as only a step in that direction. What they meant by "socialism" is open to interpretation. In June 1970, the Torres government established the Popular Assembly in an attempt to form an alternative popular government.

Consisting mainly of representatives of workers' and peasants' organizations, the Popular Assembly was intended to serve as a base for the radical transformation of economic life. However, the socialists and their allies remained divided by ideological differences and their normal obsession with power. No consensus was achieved, and many delegates, resenting the lack of power to enforce the resolutions and running short of funds, returned home frustrated.

To assert that the "Right" supports the "unlimited free market" is absurd, especially in Catholic countries. There was no movement for that sort of thing in Latin America. It's the typical amateur's attempt to impose present American realities onto a very different society. Capitalism and Marxism were both correctly seen as revolutionary doctrines and products of foreign forces. In a move the American Left has no explanation for, Torres cut the defense budget to free money for education and allowed civilian interference in strictly military matters. Clearly, rhetoric on military governments must be changed radically and the histories must be rewritten.

Torres often permitted military disobedience to go unpunished. The last step of institutional decay was a manifesto written during his last weeks by a group of junior officers who questioned his fitness. It resulted in widespread military support for the coup of August 21, 1971, by Colonel Hugo Banzer Suarez, the former Military Academy commander whom Torres had exiled.

Colonel Hugo Banzer (ruling 1971–1978), a highly respected officer who had repeatedly attempted to overthrow the Torres government, ruled for six years, the longest continuous presidential term in recent Bolivian history. Finally, stability was achieved. Banzer's presidency was characterized by unprecedented economic growth. At first he was supported by the Nationalist Popular Front *(Frente Popular Nacionalista, FPN),* an alliance between the MNR under Paz Estenssoro, who was allowed to return from exile in Lima, and the Bolivian Socialist Falange

(Falange Socialista Boliviana, FSB) under Mario Gutierrez, a more or less national socialist group. Both parties had been enemies until the chaos of the Torres system gave them a chance to change the country's direction.

During the first years of the Banzer presidency the economy improved impressively. Exports tripled between 1970 and 1974 because of increased production of petroleum, natural gas and tin, which was then refined in Bolivian smelters. The production of cotton from eastern Bolivia also tripled between 1970 and 1975. These were assisted by state funds in an import-substituting policy. He was condemned by the US and the IMF despite his success. The US rejected his economic nationalism.

The Left, seeing their issues taken from them, stepped up their violence. The government suppressed a general strike against the devaluation of the Bolivian peso in 1972. These sorts of riots were the case all over the third world at the time. In 1974, price increases for basic goods and control of food prices resulted in roadblocks by peasants in the Cochabamba Valley and their subsequent destruction by the army. It should be noted that the military had yet to nationalize the banks, the cause of this chaos.

The governing alliance disintegrated almost immediately when the MNR and the FSB split. They proved an unreliable support for Banzer because only small factions remained in the FPN. The armed forces were also divided. On June 5, 1974 younger officers belonging to the Generational Group *(Grupo Generacional)* led by General Gary Prado Salmon attempted to take over. They failed, as did another coup attempt on November 7.

The November 7, 1974 coup attempt gave Banzer the freedom he needed to cut all ties with local millionaires. When western writers refer to "civil society" or "civilian influence," this is generally what they mean, since these men control the media and most of the productive capacity of the country. Influenced by the Brazilian model, Col. Banzer announced the complete reorganization of the Bolivian political system and the formation of a "new Bolivia" under military rule. Soon, however, his economic miracle petered out due to external forces. The production of petroleum declined sharply, and *Comibol* produced at a loss, despite high mineral prices, because it was subsidizing other state agencies. Cotton production also declined when world prices fell. This is hardly the fault of the government.

The stability of the Banzer regime was superficial

because the military remained divided by personal rivalry, ideological differences, and a generational gap. Growing elite opposition was centered in the labor unions, despite the renewed military occupation of the mines. Radical students and the Roman Catholic Church became spokespersons for opposition factions, all with elite backing. There are no "spontaneous rebellions" and Bolivia is certainly no exceptions. Millionaires don't take to being silenced very well, especially when the economy begins to sputter.

The 1974 negotiation with Chile for an outlet to the sea raised expectations for an economic breakthrough. When an agreement between Banzer and Pinochet failed because of the opposition of Chilean nationalists, Banzer's position suffered. Consistently, Banzer was pressured by the US to hold elections and condemned him when he refused.

In 1977, with opposition from elite groups, military factions and pressure from the United States increasing, Banzer announced a presidential election for 1980, hoping to remain in control, but labor unrest and hostility to his regime, fanned by the US and Cuba, forced him to set the date for 1978.

General Juan Pereda, Banzer's handpicked candidate, carried out a coup in July 1978 after the National Electoral Court annulled the elections because of widespread fraud. All groups were suspected at the time, since the country was obviously not ready for elections, a fact Banzer made quite clear. Although Bolivia continued under military rule, the 1978 election marked the beginning of Bolivia's traumatic transition to liberal, elite democracy during the following four years. American elites see elections as a magic spell that confers legitimacy to winners if they are suitably liberal. Rather, elections are highly complex processes that require an advanced society capable of properly debating issues at great length without personal vendettas or memories of violence scarring the proceedings. The US wanted elections to permit the IMF and World Bank to begin dictating terms to the government, There, the new government, desperate for funds, would do whatever it took for infusions of cash, including selling the country's strategic assets. This is what "elections" mean to the west, not abstract "procedural justice."

To summarize the rule of Hugo Banzer Suarez, it might be kept in mind that he too became a politician and was elected president in 2000. However, starting from 1971, his rule introduced stability and economic growth that, had it continued, would have led to a highly prosperous Bolivia today. In a 2000 speech to the Andean Presidential Council, he stressed that power is a double edged sword. Political analysts assume that political actors seek greater and greater levels of power without noticing that, as power increases, so does the blame they must accept when things go wrong. Power is always problematic and gaining it never brings satisfaction. It's also a lot of work.

His comments in 2000 about politics being a "dirty business" suggests that political power is hardly a universal desire. If anything, the assumption that politicians want as much power as they can possible gain must be tempered with the proviso that they also seek as much power without the concomitant levels of responsibility. In other words, when responsibility grows too great, their desire for power might wane.

The phrase "banana republic" is an offensive one, and it's used in this paper with that intent. It refers to the disaster that liberal democracy usually brings to the third world. Military governments work. They work because, if the goal is to break oligarchy, then politicians dependent upon them cannot be trusted. There is simply no other institution that has both the training, the coherence and the patriotism to rule a broken country except the army. A "military dictator" is usually a laughable caricature invented by journalists too lazy to grasp the complexities of each case.

Otherwise, they're condemned by the Left for obvious reasons. It's not just that they tend to repress violent communists, but also that they steal the populist thunder from the Leftist movements that, quite often, don't believe what they preach. Any communist that says he'll grant land to the peasants can't be a communist. Marxism rejects this sort of private ownership. He's either lying or not really a communist. That this simple distinction has yet to be grasped by academics writing on this area and era should shock the reader. As far as Bolivia is concerned, under the army's rule since World War II, its average GDP growth was almost 6 percent.

He might be compared with Alfredo Stroessner, who remained popular during his very long, successful rule over Paraguay. Economic growth was substantial. He was constantly at work and was a genuine patriot, according to most accounts. He created local infrastructure and opened the country to limited foreign investment. It was only in the early 1980s, during the recession, that the army got rid of him. While this paper cannot cover everyone, the comparison between the two men is striking.

Chapter 6.
Argentina

Juan Peron can only be described in many books since his significance is so great. This will be only a brief summary of his rule. Like in all military governments, the economy did well because the state was run by men who didn't require the consent of local millionaires. From 1946 to 1953, Argentina thrived under Peron's first five-year plan. "Plans" for most military governments weren't the violent, dissociated impositions of the USSR, but general guidelines that set goals and channeled investment funds. This alone raised the ire of the American bankers.

Due to the refusal of Peron to listen to the IMF or the US, the GDP expanded by over 25 percent, about as much as it had during the previous ten years or more. The roughly 70 percent increase in fixed capital investment was accounted for mostly by industrial growth in the private sector, not government projects. Peron was yet another example of a non-liberal success story.

Economic success is never without cost. The state subsidized growth in some sectors which, in the short term, led to a wave of imports of the capital goods locals were unable to make themselves. From 1945, Argentine exports rose from $700 million to almost $2 billion. At the same time, Peron's policies led to imports that created a trade deficit just a few years later. What few economics professors will tell you is that foreign exports, in the economics of a third world state, are usually a terrible thing, since modern, experienced, wealthy corporations can easily undersell local businesses, quickly destroying them. An increase in imports, especially over many sectors, is an injection of social poison. Yet, free trade ideology is based just on that.

Peron's bid for economic independence was difficult. Great Britain owed Argentina over $650 million for agricultural supplies during the war. This was mostly in the form of Argentine Central Bank reserve notes deposited in the Bank of England. The money was useless to the Argentine government because the British ruling class was permitted to keep the money in trust. Condemning Peron as "anti-democratic" gave the British an excellent excuse to avoid paying him.

The nation's need for advanced capital goods increased, though ongoing limits on the Central Bank's access to hard currency slowed this development artificially. Argentina's currency surpluses from the war, which came to about $200 million, were made convertible to American dollars through an agreement negotiated by Central Bank President Miguel Miranda. After a short time, British Prime Minister Clement Attlee suspended this agreement. Advanced states don't pay debts to their underlings. Peron had to accept the transfer of over 15,000 miles of British-owned railways (over half the total in Argentina) instead of actual cash payment in 1948. Its almost bizarre to discuss debt obligations from a major empire to a third world state, but this situation is very instructive.

Due to ideological disputes between Peron and the US, as well as to pressure by the American agricultural lobby, Argentine foreign exchange earnings from the US collapsed, turning a $100 million surplus into a $300 million deficit. This was sheer external manipulation and imperialism. The predatory economics of neoliberalism is exactly what military governments exist to fight. These circumstances should be kept in mind today as third world governments are negotiating the same sort of debts with the developed world, though now from a position of weakness. If England figured ways around repayment and the US manipulated the currency, then why would the third world be so obligated to pay today? In fact, little of the debt the UK owed to developing countries from World War II was ever paid.

Regardless, this combined pressure wiped out the country's reserves and the state was forced to temporarily restrict the outflow of dollars to American banks. In response to this imperial arrogance, Peron authorized the nationalization of the port of Buenos Aires. This increased Argentinian control of its merchant marine by over 300 percent and eliminated the need to pay shipping fees. The Americans were furious at yet another "right wing communist/fascist" military government. Suddenly, "democracy" became an issue.

Exports fell to around $1.1 billion between 1949 and 1954, due in part to the deliberate manipulation of the terms of trade. The Central Bank was forced to devalue the peso, reducing its value by almost 75 percent in 1950. This led to a decline in capital imports. So many of the problems faced by these governments are often caused by the US and its banking elites. The goal is to maneuver governments to borrow more and more, leading to total dependency. In this case, short of bank reserves, Peron was forced to borrow $125 million from the US Export-Import Bank to cover debts. This is imperialism pure and simple. Austerity and better harvests in 1950 helped finance a recovery in 1951, but inflation went from 13 percent in 1948 to 50 percent in late 1951. A second, sharper recession soon followed created by foreign monetary warfare.

Workers' purchasing power by 1952 had declined 20 percent from its 1948 high and GDP, having exploded by 25 percent during Peron's first two years, saw zero growth from 1948 to 1952. To repeat, this was due to predatory policies from the dominant nations of the west. The Americans, of course, encouraged unions to strike, blaming the government for its own policies.

The increasing frequency of strikes, increasingly directed against Peron as the economy slid into recession in late 1954, led to the expulsion of its organizers. Peron was certain the US was trying to unseat "another fascist" and had the weapons to do so. In response, Peron called for broader constitutional reform with an elected convention that eliminated the 1853 Constitution with a new one explicitly guaranteeing social reforms. This also permitted the mass nationalization of natural resources and public services.

Undaunted by this immoral pressure from abroad,

Peron engaged in a set of stunningly large investments in Argentina's infrastructure. Investing over $100 million to modernize the railways, using parts given to the country in lieu of debt repayment by Britain. He also nationalized private airlines, creating the *Aerolíneas Argentinas* corporation in 1950. The state used the money to buy 36 new DC-3 and DC-4 aircraft and built a new international airport and a 15 mile freeway into the capital. The airport was one of the largest in the world at the time.

Peron struggled to expand the country's inadequate electric grid, which grew by about 30 percent under his postwar rule. Argentina's hydroelectric capacity increased from 45 to 350 MW during his first term to roughly about a fifth of the total public power capacity. He promoted the fossil fuel industry by ordering these resources nationalized, inaugurating *Rio Turbio* (Argentina's only active coal mine) and did the same to the state oil firm, YPF, establishing *Gas del Estado*. The 1949 completion of a gas pipeline between Comodoro Rivadavia and Buenos Aires was another significant accomplishment that didn't use foreign capital. This 1200 mile pipeline allowed natural gas production to rise quickly from 300,000 m3 to 15 million m3 daily, making the country self-sufficient in this critical area.

By contrast, the IMF and World Bank demand that foreigners control these projects in that "fair bidding" be the main method of financing. This guarantees, of course, foreign control over the country. Western powerhouses can easily undersell local actors, so its the same as granting the concession to the west. At the time, Peron's pipeline was the longest in the world. Because of this, Argentina saw an 80 percent increase in output at YPF. This led to a rise in oil production from 3.3 million m3 to over 4.8 million during Peron's tenure, but since most manufacturing was powered by generators and the number of motor vehicles grew by a third, the need for oil imports grew massively. Had the IMF had their way, the country would have been entirely hollowed out and foreign credit would have controlled all banking, leading to a purely agricultural country dedicated to export to the US. In other words, only because Argentina was run by the military that it was poised to reach first world status by this time. The US would not have this sort of competition.

Peron's military government introduced a Ministry of Health to cabinet level, led by Ramon Carrillo. The state built over 4,200 clinics and hospitals. The IMF fumed at this, demanding instead that foreign firms "compete" to take this sector over for profit. Related projects included the construction of more than 1,000 kindergartens and over 8,000 schools, including several hundred technological, nursing and teachers' schools, among an array of other public investments. These existed because the military was capable of keeping both the IMF and the local elite at bay.

The new Minister of Public Works, General Juan Pistarini, built over 650,000 new homes. The reactivation of the dormant National Mortgage Bank spurred the housing market, soon to average over eight units per 1,000 inhabitants which amounts to about 150,000 yearly. This pace was, at the time, identical to that of the US and was one of the highest rates of residential home construction in the world. Construction firms in the US hysterically demanded sanctions against the "communist/fascist" Peron who shut them out of this massive development.

To summarize, social security was made universal while education was made free to all who qualified. Working students were given one paid week before every major examination. Vast low-income housing projects were created and paid vacations, having first been introduced by Hitler's Germany in the 1930s, became standard. All workers, regardless of status, were guaranteed free medical care and half of their vacation expenses. Expecting mothers received three paid months off prior to and after giving birth. Workers' recreation centers were also constructed throughout the country. Most of these were copied from Hitler's initiatives from 1934 to 1939.

Peron was a national socialist in the best sense. His public speeches were consistently nationalist and populist. It would be difficult to separate Peronism from corporate nationalism in that he nationalized Argentina's large corporations, blurring distinctions between private enterprise and government. Such an approach was responsible for making South Korea a first world country in about 15 years under General Chung Hee Park. At the same time, the labor unions agreed to avoid strikes in exchange for a strong voice in economic planning. Since having such power is what strikes are about, the deal simply gave them their demands before they were made. Keep in mind that all socialist countries had banned labor unions. Peron minced no words and made it clear that liberalism was just "disguised plutocracy." All told, labor's share of national income went from 40 to 50 percent under his rule.

Peronism in foreign policy was strictly neutralist

and protectionist. He envisioned Argentina's role as a model for other countries in Latin America and beyond, but such ideas were ultimately abandoned, though largely out of IMF coercion. His refusal to take sides in the Cold War meant he could go to any nation he pleased for assistance if the need struck.

The simple question might be asked: does this description match up with the typical description from the average university text? Would a democratic legislature, dependent on foreign cash for their very existence, have engaged in a similar course of action? What would Argentina have looked like had the military not taken over when it did? Why are all these states, now long in the grip of the IMF, still struggling with poverty while these military governments had begun the slow conquest of these issues back in the 1960s? Have you been lied to, or do you think you "know better?"

It can hardly be denied that General Leopoldo Galtieri left quite a mark, and not just for the defeat in the Falklands. He inherited a terrible financial situation and a global recession. The Leftist press in the US called any attack on Leftist guerrillas the work of "death squads." Of the 8500 or so "disappeared," the overwhelming majority were Marxists who sympathized with the current chaos in the country they caused. These were the results of a civil war. There are no "human rights" abuses in a guerrilla war where the enemy refuses to wear uniforms. The only reason the Americans went wild was that the communists were under attack.

Prior to his rule, in the later 1970s, the military issued this proclamation:

> Our people have suffered a new frustration. Faced with a tremendous power vacuum, one which is capable of plunging us into dissolution and anarchy; the lack of integral policy shown by the National Government; the repeated and successive contradictions evidenced by the adoption of incoherent measures of all kinds; in the absence of a comprehensive strategy which, led by political power, it can face subversion; the lack of solutions to basic problems of political extremism; the total absence of the ethical and moral examples to be given by

those who exercise leadership in the state; a
manifest irresponsibility in the management
of the economy that would lead to the
exhaustion of our productive capacity; to
widespread speculation and corruption, all
of which translates into an irreparable loss
of the sense of greatness and of faith: the
Armed Forces, fulfilling an obligation they
have granted to them, have assumed the
leadership of the state (Proclamation of the
Army, March 1976).

This was the announcement of the military
takeover. It was done, as the junta mentions, under the
harshest of conditions and with a government that was too
weak to take action against a mounting civil war. The CIA
reported that the first six months of the "National
Reorganization Process" were highly successful both
politically and economically. Inflation was reduced and
unemployment dropped substantially. The "People's
Revolutionary Army" was the Leftist terror unit that forced
the reaction of the Argentinian state. They were simply
fighting an extremely violent and well-protected

communist insurgency.

The military published its own rationale for taking over:

> The basic objectives to be achieved during the process to ensure the subsequent realization of effective democracy and according to national reality, they are:
> 2 1 . Realization of political sovereignty based on action of revitalized constitutional institutions, which permanently place national interest above any sectarianism, tendency or personalism.
> 2.2. Validity of the values of Christian morality, national tradition and the dignity of the Argentine being.
> 2.3. National security is effective, eliminating subversion and the causes that favor its existence.
> 2.4. Full force will be placed behind the legal and social order.
> 2.5. Implementation of a socioeconomic program to ensure national self-ownership

and full realization of the Argentine man;
where the state maintains control over vital
areas needed for security and development
and provide initiative and private capital,
national and foreign wealth with a smooth
participation in the process of rational
exploitation of resources, neutralizing any
possibility of interference by outsiders.

2.6. Achieving general well-being through
fruitful work, with equal opportunities and
an adequate sense of social justice.

2.7. Harmonious relationship between state,
capital and labor, with strengthened
development of the business and trade union
structures, adjusted to their specific
purposes.

2.8. Establishment of an educational system
in line with the the need for the country to
serve effectively the objectives of the
convention and to consolidate values and
aspirations of our culture.

2.9. To maintain an international presence in
the western and Christian world, proving the

capacity for self-determination; and ensuring
the strengthening of the Argentine
significance in the concert of nations.

The junta came to power then, with a very explicit
sense of itself. There can be no doubt that the constitutional
order could not deal with both civil war and economic
implosion. The Army's position continues in "Section
Three: Ideas Governing the Intervention of the Army in
National Politics"

The historical justification for the
intervention of the military in the national
government lies exclusively in that normal
functioning does not offer any security as
regards the maintenance of national
integrity and the location of the country
with respect to its destiny. Having accepted
this premise, it is particularly important to
clearly define the guiding ideas – the
philosophy – that underpins this
intervention and its operational modality.
In order for these basic aspects to be fully

91

understood and to be carried out with absolute unity of criteria, all the elements that make up the current situation in the country must be objectively visualized, this is misrule, administrative chaos, venality, but also the existence of strong political currents; a working class that's active and has not yet turned to Marxism; with a church ready to support the process but ready to denounce any excess against dignity; with a cry for exemplary punishment but as long as the sector to which it belongs is not affected; at last, with the international environment that in principle will not be favorable to the interruption of institutional continuity and that it will adjust its subsequent attitude to this action of the army in the pursuit of social, economic and administrative and efficiency that your government demonstrates.

Keeping the situation constantly in mind, starting and the ultimate goal to be achieved, specified in [the above] and that is nothing other than the establishment of a truly representative democracy, with full force of our traditional Republican principles, with an authentic and effective federalism, supported by currents of broad national opinion and only motivated by the greatness of the country and the common good, based on a society united, organized and supportive and with a vigorous economy in order to allow the full individual and social realization of Argentina, the guiding ideas that encourage the intervention of the [military] will be defined at this juncture and its mode fundamental operational (Bases, 1976, from the Spanish).

This extensive concept is rarely spoken of in treatments of military governments. The caricature of academic work on the subject makes a mockery of the complexity involved. The CIA document "Six Months of the Argentinian Military Government" condemns "human rights abuses" in no uncertain terms. While praising the army for its success economically, anti-communist vigilantes (not the government) were responsible for these "abuses" and were "putting a strain on the relationship between the two countries."

Yet, it was only because of this "Dirty War" that the Argentinian state was victorious over these terrorists. They Left were terrorists in that they targeted civilians, wore no uniforms and rejected any compromise with the state. The American press came resolutely down on their side, as always.

In the "Memorandum of Conversation" between the Argentinian foreign minister and Undersecretary of State Phillip Habib in October of 1978, its very clear that the US considered Argentina to be fighting a civil war and not engaging in "terror" for the fun of it. Argentina had declared victory over the Leftists, which enraged the American elite.

The foreign minister mentions that the communists had begun a campaign to accuse the military of being "Anti-Jewish." This was recorded without criticism by the world press. As it turns out, this government was pro-Israel, but the knee-jerk accusation against anti-communism

94

perhaps revealed more than the writer meant to. Also, the US threatened the minister with vetoing two loans from the Export-Import Bank to Argentina if this "terror" didn't stop. The press still today pretends that the US "supported" the dictatorship there, yet the documents prove it did no such thing and, conveniently, never defines the term "support." General Galiteri was acquitted of all "crimes" by an international court backed by the US that had no jurisdiction over Argentina. He fell because of the defeat in the Falklands War.

Over and over again the US State Department and CIA condemn Argentina for its fighting a civil war. In no manner did the US deviate from this position. It only rarely talks about the most pressing issue, the economy. In the late 1970s, of course, the world was in a grip of an oil-induced depression. Argentina was not immune.

In 1977 however, new construction in the country went up by 35 percent while investment in mechanical capital went up by over 50 percent. The following year saw negative growth, but it rebounded by 1980. Unfortunately, the junta engaged in pro-IMF policies that soon harmed the country, as they always do. The economy moved from one of industrial and agricultural production to profits based on

95

non-productive financial speculation given the inflation problem and its effect on bonds.

The '80s proved a decade of stagnation in the Latin American economies. Argentine inflation was the highest in the world during the period 1976-1984 with a 1983 inflation rate of almost 1000 percent. The country, after the Falklands disaster, saw its earlier gains vanish while the junta needed to support US neoliberal goals or forego loans. Small and medium-sized factories were hit hard and the currency collapsed.

The foreign capital entering Argentina wasn't productive, by and large, and was speculative in nature. Financial instruments were the profit-machine of choice. This closely integrated Argentina with the transnational financial market and provided a new indirect form of appropriation of surpluses: the transfer to the state of a large part of its significant external indebtedness. By following American dictates, the economy suffered and capital fled the country. Of the total Argentine external debt in 1983, 89 percent corresponded to financial debt (Azpiazu, 1983 and Azpiazu, 1988).

Yet, under both military governments, Argentina was a successful state. State control of industry, import substitution, a strong national religion, state control of banking and limited planning has worked in these countries whenever its been tried. Its only been outside forces that sought to destroy it, usually the USA.

Chapter 7.
Chile

Almost nothing praising the reign of Augusto Pinochet exists in English, including from the US government that allegedly "supported" him. With no evidence or statistics, the ruling class of the western world declared this man one of the most evil in recent history. Is this true? Again, the term "support" merely means that sanctions weren't placed on the country. Trade went as planned. Minimal military aid existed for all Chilean governments, frozen only under Pinochet.

On September 11 1973, the Chilean military ousted the sort-of socialist Allende government. In less than 24 hours, the armed forces had consolidated control of the country. In the tense early period of the military regime it was not uncommon for civilians falsely to accuse individuals of being armed leftists in order to settle private scores, but most of the people killed by the military were part of the of the armed Left, but this is exactly why the ruling class gets so upset with men like him. No government randomly killed people. There was always a military or political reason.

Democracy, wherever it goes, needs to be imposed

at the barrel of a gun – France in 1789, England under Cromwell, China under Sun, Russia under Kerensky, Iraq under whoever Fox news says is in charge, Serbia under the DOSies, and many others. Why is killing of "innocents" bad in Chile, but good (or at least neutral) in France around 1789? And how do we know they're innocent?

Pinochet did not pretend to be an intellectual or even a leader (he brought in Americans to teach him about economics). Like Franco in Spain or Assad in Syria, he did what he was forced to do. He did not want power nor did he seek it. Even more, why does the Left/neo-right establishment claim Allende was legitimate because he was elected? Was not ARENA in El Salvador elected as well? Wasn't Putin? Wasn't Lukashenko? At least, those people received more than the 36.3 percent Allende received. Without a run-off system, the Chilean system simply gave the presidency to the plurality winner, but this, to the tenured professor in the Ivy Leagues, is a "massive mandate from 'the people' to institute socialism," to paraphrase Eric Hobsbawm, or someone like that.

The following is from the February 1999 edition of *Liberty*, and was written by John Cobin and Karen Araujo. Now, I have never heard of *Liberty* before, but I assume its some Libertarian group because they always seem to have periodicals with "Liberty" somewhere in the title.

The world rarely quiets itself from wars and other conflicts, and few wars can be called just from a classically liberal perspective. Like America's War for Independence and the War Between the States, Chile's struggle against the communists was a just conflict. The revolution in Chile was an act of self defense against legal looters and armed bandits. As is inevitable in any war, errors were made and innocent lives lost. But despite its mistakes, the revolution Left a positive legacy: Chile has a free and prosperous economy and stable republican institutions. This is the context in which the British arrest of General Augusto Pinochet, the leader of Chile's revolution, must be judged. When Pinochet took over, Chile was experiencing a rapid decay in the quality of life. Salvador Allende had been elected president victory in a three-way election, in

which he won a minority of the vote [36.3%
in an election decided by the legislature] and
immediately set about making himself into
the dictator of a socialist country. There
were reports of Allende killing dozens or
even hundreds of people in the countryside.
He was stealing and nationalizing private
property. There was 1,000 percent inflation
during his 1,000 days of rule. There was
much hunger (for those who were not "in"
with the socialists) and it was not
uncommon to see people without shoes.

Now, if the US was "supporting" Pinochet, why did
the Regime not bother to mention Allende's killings? In
fact, why did the government not write papers and books
explaining his success? Why didn't the State Department or
the CIA bring the many Chilean writers who backed
Pinochet to the US and translate their works into English?
Why, when he was banned from the US in the 1970s, were
Soviet technicians invited to study at MIT? Why were these
simple questions never asked?

The authors continue:

Hector Hevia, a Chilean professor who lived through those chaotic times recalls, "You had to wait in line for hours to get a piece of meat you could not eat." By July 1973, Allende had centralized control of nearly everything, including replacing the top two men in every firm with a bureaucrat. In short, Allende was destroying people's lives, and Chileans had a right to defend themselves against him. . . .There were massive demonstrations calling for Allende's resignation. On August 22, 1973, the Chilean chamber of deputies passed a resolution of censure against Allende. Congressional deputies condemned him and his government for violating the constitution and the law in order to "institute a totalitarian system absolutely opposed to the representative system of government that the Constitution establishes," and called upon the military to intervene. . . According to the report of the respected Rettig Commission of the democratic Aylwin government, there were 1,173 deaths, including military personnel, both during the revolution and in its aftermath, from September to December 1973. *The Rettig Commission reported a total of 2,033 deaths perpetrated by the military during their 17-years of rule, and 265 deaths of military personnel, civilians killed by terrorists, and deaths due to general political violence.* The deaths are under-counted on both sides, and the number of people who disappeared are included in the total. The majority–63 percent–of those killed were members of Marxist political parties, such as in the Movement of the Revolutionary Left, an entirely terrorist group, the Manuel Rodriguez Front, entirely terrorist, the Socialist and Communist parties, both of which had armed contingents, and of smaller, violent Marxist parties. Sola Sierra, president of the Group of the Relatives of the Arrested-Disappeared in Chile, herself a communist, stated that the

103

percentage of people killed who were affiliated with Marxist parties was actually much higher, since relatives often feared to publicly reveal the political affiliation of the dead (emphasis mine).

Please keep in mind that these Marxist parties, if they had succeeded, would, as per their very public program, have set up a totalitarian state, tightly censored the media, destroyed the economy, set up forced labor camps and engaged in mass executions. Every single Marxist state has done these things without exception.

Now, the British have arrested Pinochet at the request of a Spanish court, seeking to prosecute him for various offenses committed during the revolution. He stands accused of genocide and murder, and everyone knows that. Western news media seldom reported the terrorist activities of the communists that Pinochet fought, and Pinochet gets little sympathy in Europe or North America. . . .

104

Here, the authors are wrong: the communist terrorists in Latin America are never – rather than seldom – held responsible for their actions, which, at last count, are well over 100 million corpses. As many who perpetrated these crimes are still alive, the irony and mockery here is bitter. This is from a journalist in Santiago.

Things are very different here in Chile. Most people we have talked to are uneasy, sad, and even outraged about the arrest [of Pinochet]. Recent polls put popular support in Chile for Pinochet's release at over 75 percent. Alvaro Vial, academic Vice President at Finis Terrae University, who frequently writes on Chilean political issues for the national press, said that he believes that perhaps 40 percent of Chileans would firmly stand behind Pinochet. Then there are probably another 30 to 40 percent who support his return to Chile. . . The vast majority of Chileans want Pinochet to be freed. There are frequent pro-Pinochet demonstrations in front of the British and Spanish embassies which sometimes turn violent, as demonstrations here often do. The boulevard in front of the Spanish embassy is at times sealed off and that embassy, along with the British Ambassador's residence, are continually barricaded. We think Pinochet's supporters in Chile have a good point. To charge Pinochet with murder would be as unjust as charging Patrick Henry or Thomas Jefferson with murdering Redcoats or with accidentally shooting a neighbor while trying to kill a Redcoat. All such revolutionaries act in self defense against an oppressive state, and thus their cause is just, despite tragedies and accidental loss of innocent lives that might occur. The media in the United States and in Europe have distorted the facts regarding Pinochet. He stands accused of murder and crimes against humanity, and that is the beginning and the end of the story as far as most journalists are concerned. But CNN and of the international

106

news media rarely reveal details about the terrorist activities of the communists that Pinochet was fighting. Because of their mostly Leftist bias, most media do not sympathize with Pinochet, or with his revolution against armed socialists who pushed the country to civil war. Thus, the media portray Pinochet as a senseless and brutal dictator and ignore the circumstances in which Pinochet assumed power: to prevent a bloody, protracted civil war. Pinochet, and those under his command, almost certainly were responsible for the death of innocent people. In the chaos and confusion of war, such tragedies are inevitable. Those outside the fray would do well to hesitate to pass judgment on the fallible human beings swept up in the vortex of war. Pinochet was not pure; no one could be, ever has been, or ever will be under such circumstances.

Pinochet carried out an economic and political revolution that successively

devolved power away from the state.
Afterward he voluntarily stepped down from
power. In doing so, his successors agreed to
give him immunity from prosecution for
misdeeds committed during the revolution.
To us, this seems like a reasonable
arrangement; the revolution was over, peace,
prosperity, and a stable republic stood in the
place of chaos, poverty and dictatorship. . . .
Pinochet was no tyrant. Do tyrants usher in
more freedom? Do they relinquish their
power voluntarily? Pinochet did both. What
an absurd precedent Pinochet's arrest sets.
Monsters like Zaire's Mobutu, Cambodia's
Pol Pot, and most of the dictators of the
communist countries of eastern Europe were
not harangued by world tribunals and the
press. But Pinochet, who voluntarily stepped
down from office and now continues to
serve his country as a member of its Senate,
is arrested when he visits Britain!

Can you think of a major, armed event in politics

where innocent people weren't killed? And again, who is "innocent?" It's ridiculous for academics and journalists to take advantage of public ignorance to demand, when military governments are concerned, they prosecute a civil war without bloodshed. For obvious reasons, these people set impossible standards for their enemies, but glory in the carnage of their friends. As the whole point of scholarship is to rise above these petty pleadings and see the truth hidden in the rhetoric, they fail to do their job, at least as its normally defined.

The fact is that they don't want to learn is that bloodshed – lots of it – is inherently part of Leftist political ideology, especially Marxism. Its actually a theoretical necessity. On the Right, its merely an unfortunate byproduct of the fact that they're not perfect and their enemies often don't wear uniforms. Furthermore, during such violent events, the use of the term "innocent" is non-empirical and is merely a rhetorical symbol. What it seems to mean is that "non-combatants" are killed, which could also just mean communists in jeans rather than fatigues. They have no way of knowing if these people are "innocent" or not. No government of this type, struggling for legitimacy and popularity (as well as being notoriously poor in propaganda), would begin killing random people. Yet even this simple point is beyond the capacity of the Ivy League millionaires.

Lets look at the figures. This author has made the following argument since he was a teenager: In general, military governments, when properly motivated, outperform democratic ones in terms of economic growth. This is clear in Taiwan, South Korea, Thailand, and authoritarian China (i.e. the formerly communist China). Now, unsurprisingly, it is difficult to get a solid statistical reading on Chile during Pinochet's rule, due to his massive successes, and due to the US banks' desire to repress them. There is very little in terms of statistics during his era – for obvious reasons, but occasionally, the World Bank will let a few squeaks out.

The pseudo-intellectual journalists suffer badly with cognitive dissonance: Pinochet was bad/wages skyrocketed; Pinochet was bad/all economic indicators went through he roof; Pinochet was bad/infant mortality almost became non-existent. We can't envy them. These conflicts normally are resolved by ad hominem attacks, threatening me, and demanding higher salaries. As Regime supporters can't deal with the fact that militaries rule far better than democracies, they merely "deny-and-ban," the typical "liberal-democratic" two-step. According to the World Bank, the GNP of the country between 1975 and 1990 rose from 35 billion (Chilean) pesos to a whopping nine trillion. A massive increase.

Interestingly, the official statistics coming from American academics make the claim, repeated in a very bad book by Elton Rayack, that the GDP only went up just a bit over one percent yearly from 1975 to 1980. These bogus statistics are normally repeated on Marxist websites and academic journals. These people have cooked the books in order to make their a priori commitments to "democracy" work out (and you'll also notice that those who hate Pinochet will use statistics from his book or those copying from him. They won't touch the World Bank numbers). The World Bank, measuring in dollars, claims that the economy increased by about eight percent yearly, on average. This was done at a time of financial meltdown throughout Latin America, inflation out of control throughout the continent, and is being figured by an institution that has been nothing but hostile to Pinochet and all like him.

Chile under Pinochet developed one of the highest

savings rates in the world, bested only by Japan. Political writer Piero Scaruffi has put in this way:

> The truth is that Pinochet's coup against Allende was welcomed by many, as any visitor to Chile in those years can report. The Christian Democrats, the largest party in Chile, approved the coup, albeit with reservations. Patricio Aylwin (who would become Chile's first democratically elected president after Pinochet's resignations) thanked the army for "saving Chile's democracy." Students and workers were persecuted, and the methods cannot be excused. But there is also no doubt that Chile's economy started reviving almost immediately, and within a few years it overtook all the economies of South America. Chile came to be called "the Switzerland of Latin America," thanks to its cleanliness, efficiency and (relative) wealth. So much so, that today most Latin-American economies are clearly inspired by Pinochet's

112

experiment, and the leader of neighboring Peru, Fujimori, has clearly replicated Pinochet's authoritarian strategies (with equal success, at least initially). While the West was flooded by communist propaganda describing Chile as hell, Pinochet was probably enjoying the highest approval rate in the whole of Latin America. He is the only dictator in modern history who let people vote against him. It is now clear that Pinochet was convinced of winning that referendum. He lost it by a very narrow margin. Two or three years earlier, when Chileans were still afraid of a revival of communism, he would have won it. Proof is that Allende's disciples have lost all elections since the return to democracy. Over and over again, Chileans have voted to keep the leftists out of the government. It appears that, 30 years later, the Left is finally capable of facing its guilt, not only of exposing Pinochet's guilt.

Only the most brutal of dictators leave their countries with a large trade surpluses, it seems. From 1985 to 1995, the overall volume of trade rose from $3 billion to over $16 billion. Pinochet's brutality left Chile with the lowest infant mortality rate in Latin America, with a shocking score of eight (per 1,000 live births) against 27 for the rest of the continent (the US stands at about seven, England, about 5.5), and about where Chile stood at the dawn of the Allende government.

Pinochet's brutality saved countless lives. The country enjoyed a literacy rate of 96 percent at the end of his reign of terror. As soon as he left office in 1990, Chile went into a tailspin, suffering a catastrophic recession, where its GDP growth for the next two years or so went to nearly zero. Inflation was brought under control only by the military, and thus left the subsequent governments an excellent legacy to build upon, and helps explain the general's continual popularity in the country today.

Pinochet did not "clamp down on political dissent." This is another myth of the faculty lounge scribblers: he liquidated Marxist organizations who would have done to Chile what they did in China. Destroying Leninist groups by any means necessary is an act done to preserve "human

114

rights," not destroy it. Yet, from the comfort of their air conditioned offices, well paid professors have the gall to tell a general how to deal with civil unrest. Civil society was robust under the general, and only Leninists were proscribed and prosecuted. This is a government's obligation and Pinochet did it well. If he is a "brutal dictator," then brutal dictators are the saviors of Latin America.

Conclusions

Today, the record of the American-backed banana republics is a pathetic, pitiable sight. The President of Argentina Mauricio Macri has been begging the IMF for a new loan of $50 billion. The program of financial assistance to Buenos Aires ends in December 2019. No one denies that, in truth, this is the date of another default, which will continue to hollow out Argentina and destroy whatever independence she ever had. This year, inflation in Argentina will reach 32 percent, although the government promised no more than 15.7 percent. Keep in mind that this comes from the most optimistic forecast. GDP instead of the expected growth of 3.2 percent will decline, at best, by one percent.

Now the main task of the president, like any democratic politician, is to survive the next election, which will take place in 2019. As American banks slowly take over the country entirely, the president deflects attention from this and says that thanks to the next IMF loan, investors will believe in the country's solvency and return to Argentina with money. Under liberal democracy, when a country's debt gets too high, all its property is bought for pennies on the peso and national sovereignty is a memory. This is the universal legacy of democracy in this part of the world. In the 1990s, Domingo Cavallo, the Minister for Foreign Affairs, in a panic, was forced to link the peso to the dollar, announced the massive privatization of state property and freed foreign investors from taxes for a period of five to 25 years. This is what democracy brings. It failed.

By 2000, Argentine national companies had by that time been broken by foreign competitors, and, as a result, by 2001 the local elites were faced with overdue bond payments, which meant creditors had to write off this worthless paper. The IMF then cut its losses. In other words, it's strip mining born out of a total lack of confidence. Twenty years ago during the Asian meltdown, those economies with a state controlled central bank were the only ones to survive. The most illustrative case is South Korea after the speculative bubble created by Soros burst. In exchange for a loan of $60 billion, the government agreed to sell to foreign companies the assets of its two largest banks and to allow foreign financial organizations the right to conduct transactions in the country without restrictions. General Park's miracle was reversed and Korea became an economic protectorate of the US.

In addition, Korea lifted the ban on the sale of land to foreigners and eliminated the traditional form of production that plagued transnational corporations – the "*chaebol*" system – which accounted for almost a third of GDP. This system was designed to keep foreign companies out and organizing local capital in such sizes that the west would have a fight if it sought to unseat them. They found a way around it.

The economy was restored, but now it is almost entirely controlled by American capital. This is the nature of the "free market" and globalization in world affairs. Years ago, the military from all over the continent were aware of this, and rushed in to keep it from continuing. They were denounced by the US and replaced with weak republics that are easy to manipulate. Liberal democracy is inherently imperial.

The American policy towards military governments have been almost universally hostile. In 1959, the goals of the NSC were laid out:

> Foster close military relations with the Latin
> American armed forces in order to increase
> their understanding of, and orientation

118

toward, U.S. objectives and policies, and to promote democratic concepts and foster pro-American sentiments among Latin American military personnel. (National Security Council Report, NSC 5902/1, 1959, 52).

This couldn't be clearer. This wasn't meant for public consumption, so its the official government position. In that document, the key section is here:

Relationship of the United States to "dictatorial" and "democratic" governments. Closely allied to rising popular desires for more democratic governments and the difficulties which Latin America has generally continued to find in establishing viable, representative regimes is the phenomenon that much of Latin American opinion holds the United States responsible in an important degree for the area's dictatorial regimes on the grounds that U.S. military and economic cooperation, diplomatic recognition and/or

119

other evidences of support contribute significantly to such regimes' ability to stay in power. The inference is drawn that the United States is, at best, disinterested in the development of democracy in the area and, less charitably, that the United States on balance favors authoritarian regimes as providing greater stability, greater resistance to Communist penetration and a better climate for U.S. economic interests. However, a departure *from the historic U.S. policy of maintaining relations with all governments of the area regardless of political complexion* would imply a departure from our obligation not to intervene in internal affairs, a policy to which Latin Americans attach equal or greater importance than to their desire for U.S. *assistance in the elimination of unpopular dictatorial regimes. In the past the United States has intervened in the internal affairs of other American states in support of democratic and against dictatorial elements, but these efforts have been ineffectual and even counter-productive.* They have often brought the condemnation of the partisans of both elements upon the United States. It is, however, possible for the United States within the limits of nonintervention to pursue a policy of encouraging those governments which have a genuinely popular base and are effectively striving towards the establishment of representative and democratic governments, *while maintaining correct diplomatic and other relations with other recognized governments as may be necessary to safeguard the national interest* (emphasis mine).

The popular mythology of American policy in Latin American is, like everything else, based on myths enforced by repetition. To deny the myth is to put one's career at risk. This author can attest to this clearly. Truth isn't a defense, only the defense of the narrative is.

On Sunday, October 6, 1963, the *New York Herald*

Tribune published an article by Assistant Secretary of State for Inter-American Affairs Edwin Martin that outlined U.S. policy toward military governments in Latin America. In the piece, he emphasized American support for "constitutional civilian governments" in the region. He stated that the military in Latin America must play an "active and constructive role" in support of these governments. Martin noted further that the militaries of some Latin American nations had "played critical roles" in dislodging dictators from power, instituting progressive reforms, and returning their countries to more democratic civilian control.

Still, Martin continued, military governments must be condemned as anti-democratic. He cautioned that the United States could not be expected to intervene militarily or economically against any military government in the region established by coup d'etat. Rather, it was the responsibility of the Latin Americans themselves to create conditions in which such regimes could not survive and in which democracy could prosper. This is a mystification. He's referring to local elites. The text of the article is in *Department of State Bulletin,* November 4, 1963, pages 698-700. It was repeated to all Latin American diplomatic posts in Department of State Circular 637, which described it as having been cleared "at highest levels" of the U.S. Government. (Kennedy Library, National Security Files, Regional Security Series, Latin America, July-November 1963).

A July 14 article in *The New York Times* quoted Department of State officials as lauding the "sense of mission" displayed by the Ecuadorean military when it overthrew the Arosemena government in 1963, a government which had opposed many American demands. The article caused worry among Latin American elites and prompted a concerned letter from Venezuelan President Romulo Betancourt to President Kennedy which was delivered personally by the Venezuelan ambassador in August (Department of State, Central Files, POL 26 LAT AM). President Kennedy, in his reply, assured the Venezuelan president that the State Department officials had been misquoted and that it was the "unalterable position of the Government of the United States to support representative, constitutional processes" in Latin America (Ibid.).

In 1969, an Intelligence Memorandum, not meant for the public, reads:

The military regimes, again like their civilian counterparts, believe that the US has dominated Latin America too long and that part of the solution to this problem is a broadening of contacts with the rest of the world, including the Communist bloc. This was once anathema to the Latins, especially to the military, who foresaw increased security problems, an influx of Communist propaganda, and the prospect that domestic Communists would be strengthened. The view in many countries has changed somewhat, although there are still a few, primarily in Central America, remain convinced that expanded contacts would open a floodgate of Communist inroads. With the slowdown of pressure from Castro and of his open support for domestic guerrillas or terrorists, military as well civilian leaders who see less danger from this direction. Thus, the avowedly anti-Communist military in Peru and Bolivia

now seem prepared to expand their contacts
with Cuba as well as with the bloc
(Intelligence Memorandum, OCI No.
2622/69, Washington, December 8, 1969.
The Military and Nationalism in Latin
America, emphasis mine).

All of these seem to fly in the face of journalistic
assumptions and TV talking head axioms. None of their
historical analysis is true. The American intelligence
community in 1969, during the height of the Vietnam War,
is chiding the military in these countries for unnecessarily
fearing communist subversion of their countries. How can
this be explained? The typical histories of the era needs to
be rewritten.

Contrary to myth, there was no real "embargo" on
Cuba or Nicaragua. The Cuban law itself permitted so
many exceptions that it seems almost designed to
encourage evasion. Court cases against lawbreakers were
drawn out and expensive given the vague wording of the
law and the laundry list of excepted goods, not to mention
goods bought from Canada and western Europe. The

"sanctions" were irrelevant and had symbolic value only. No president can tell elite billionaires where they can and cannot make more money. It was a symbolic piece of paper that, when removed by Obama, led to only slight changes in the Cuban economy.

The foundational truth here is that the US is controlled by well-organized corporate interests. They seek profit, but more than this, to create an ideological disposition of the population that would justify their rule. They know they have no right to rule, so they rely on manipulation. This means the destruction of alternative loyalties to things like family, nation and class that serve as an emotional and social foundation for rebellion. Its the emotional and social foundation for anything. The creation of confusion and relativism create aboulia, and lead to cynicism and inaction. Over time, stress, confusion and state weakness lead to a social order that's severed from its past and seeks only short term survival. Its what capitalism requires to function.

Liberalism is the official ideology of the American ruling class. "Liberalism" here refers to capitalist economic assumptions, egocentrism, feminism, free abortion, easy divorce, legal pornography and a flood of western produced "cultural" objects forcefully imposed on the world, all of which enrich corporate bosses. None of these can be separated from another. The WTO forbids any country to keep western porn or other elite media projects out of the country. Western media soon crowds out the local with its superior resources and the mind of the nation is dictated from abroad.

To call a military government "right wing" is only true in the older, European sense of the term. These were all national socialist states in the broad sense. Capitalism was distrusted and, without exception, nationalism and import substitution were the main policy guidelines that created strong growth. Traditionally, conservatism, properly understood, is typified by hierarchy, agrarianism, small landowners, ethnonationalism, import substitution, a strong church, sometimes militarism, anticommunism (but not antisocialism), idealism and a strong emphasis on the extended family. In all cases without exception, the military governments of Latin America were conservative in this older, truer sense. In American politics, "conservatism" is a misnomer. It is really libertarianism.

Military governments and nationalist states worldwide have been immensely successful economically.

They all created local investor confidence, national prosperity, the growth of domestic demand, the rejection of the IMF and backed a strategic, state-subsidized industrialization. For this reason among others, the US condemned these governments. For the Leftist still under the illusion the US "backed" governments like this, how do they explain why the US would "support" policies that led to the mass nationalization of strategic industries? This prejudice exists because of repetition, the almost non-existent apologetic literature in English and pure force. This book is one of the only published works defending these men and military governments in general. These government were more reformist, representative and fair than the alternatives.

This essay, finally, has proven what its set out to show: military governments were the only guard against the total hollowing-out of Latin American economies to either communist revolution on the one hand or liberal capitalist exploitation on the other. The limited ideological vocabulary of the US military and intelligence community prove an embarrassing, obtuse establishment incapable of understanding that national socialism (not Hitlerism) is a viable and successful form of government. Yet, the US

128

served the interest of western capital and the prosperity of Latin American societies was never an issue. They didn't answer to the military of Bolivia, they answered to the major banks that floated the loans which kept the US functioning.

Unfortunately, the successes of these states have all been undone when the IMF-supported banana republics were restored. Argentina and Peru were close to first world status when their militaries were forced out. In 2019, Latin America remains in poverty and crime; as they're drowning in drugs in the name of "democracy" and "human rights." Regardless whether Leftists, "socialists," or free marketeers were in positions of power, the results are all the same. Capitalist and communist governments create ignorance, dependency and lead to irrational results that benefit foreign elites. Buzzwords and prejudice have led to the destruction of a whole continent. Ideological and historical ignorance have led to the destruction of Latin America's hard won independence, rendering it today a sham. It's time for the stupidity to end. Liberal democracy is a fraud.

Select Bibliography:

These are basic sources on the question. Almost all of these repeat the same discredited arguments this paper was designed to refute. Sources cited in-text are not listed here.

Alexander, RJ (2007) A History of Organized Labor in Peru and Ecuador. Praeger

McSherry, J. Patrice (2011) Industrial Repression and Operation Condor in Latin America. In Esparza, Marcia, Henry R. Huttenbach and Daniel Feierstein eds: State Violence and Genocide in Latin America: The Cold War Years. Routledge

Green, John (2015) History of Political Murder in Latin America: Killing the Messengers of Change by John Green SUNY Press

McSherry, J. Patrice (2002) Tracking the Origins of a State Terror Network: Operation Condor. Latin American Perspectives. 29 (1): 36–60
(She seems unable to track actual terror networks. States aren't hard to "track," since they're public institutions. What an idiot).

Grandin, Greg (2011) The Last Colonial Massacre: Latin America in the Cold War. University of Chicago Press

Hixson, Walter L. (2009) The Myth of American Diplomacy: National Identity and U.S. Foreign Policy. Yale University Press

Rohter, Larry (January 24, 2014) Exposing the Legacy of

Operation Condor. The New York Times (He exposes nothing but his lack of research skills and writing ability).

Stanley, Ruth (2006) Predatory States: Operation Condor and Covert War in Latin America
(What is it with women in corny, overly dramatic titles?)

Black, Jan Knippers (1977) United States Penetration of Brazil. Manchester University Press
(I'm sure he means it in the metaphorical sense)

Languth, A.J. (1978) Hidden Terrors. Pantheon Books

Melvyn P and OA Westad (2000) The Cambridge History of the Cold War (Volume 3). Cambridge University Press

Lewis, Paul (1990) The Crisis of Argentine Capitalism. University of North Carolina Press

Argentina: From Insolvency to Growth, World Bank Press, 1993

Colby, Jason M (2015) Reagan and Central America. In Andrew L. Johns, ed. A Companion to Ronald Reagan, 411-433

Gilderhus, Mark T (1999). The Second Century: US-Latin American Relations Since 1889.

Horwitz, Betty, and Bruce M. Bagley (2016). Latin America and the Caribbean in the Global Context: Why Care about the Americas? Routledge

LaRosa, Michael and Frank Mora, eds (2006) Neighborly

Adversaries: Readings in US–Latin American Relations.
Colombia

Menjivar, Cecilia, and Nestor Rodriguez, eds (2005) When
States Kill: Latin America, the U.S., and Technologies of
Terror. University of Texas Press
("When States Kill" received the Denise Leith Airhead
award for the worst and most corny title in 2018. Its the
only interesting thing about this book).

Rivas, Darlene (2008) United States–Latin American
Relations, 1942–1960. in Robert Schulzinger, ed., A
Companion to American Foreign Relations 230-54

LaFeber, Walter (1993). Inevitable Revolutions: The
United States in Central America. W. W. Norton and
Company

Latin American Studies Association (1984). The Electoral
Process in Nicaragua: Domestic and International
Influences.

Grandin, Greg (2006). Empire's Workshop: Latin America,
the United States, and the Rise of the New Imperialism.
Macmillan

Hamilton, Lee H and DK Inouye (1995). Report of the
Congressional Committees Investigating the Iran/Contra
Affair. DIANE Publishing

Carothers, Thomas (1993) In the Name of Democracy: U.S.
Policy Toward Latin America in the Reagan Years.
University of California Press

McClintock, Michael (1992) Instruments of Statecraft: U.S. Guerrilla Warfare, Counter-Insurgency, Counter-Terrorism, 1940–1990. Pantheon Books

Stokes, Doug (2004) America's Other War: Terrorizing Colombia. Zed Books
(Another stupid title. The US is involved in at least four or five wars at the same time. There are lots of "other wars").

CIA Document 603 from September 30 1976 "First Six Months of the Argentinian Military Dictatorship."
https://nsarchive2.gwu.edu//NSAEBB/NSAEBB104/Doc3%20760930.pdf

US Department of State. Secretary's Meeting with Argentine Foreign Minister Guzzetti, October 7, 1976. Document P8-20118-1700

Azpiazu, D. (1988) The New Economic Power. Buenos Aires. Hyspamérica 1988.

Azpiazu, D. (1983) The Structure of Markets and the Deindustrialization of Argentina 1976-1983 . Buenos Aires. Center for Transnational Economy

Baccaria, L (1985) The Evolution of Employment and Wages in the Short Term. The Argentine Case 1970-1983. ECLAC

Bases Politicas de las FF-AA Para el Proceso de Reorgaization Nacional. Military Junta of Argentina, 1979 (in Spanish)
http://www.ruinasdigitales.com/revistas/dictadura/Dictadura%20-

%20Documentos%20Basicos%20y%20Bases%20Politicas.
pdf